PRAISE FOR

BUILDING A FAMILY OF FAITH

Andy Dooley has found a creative and engaging way to restore the value of family time that is centered around God's Word and making it relatable, fun, and engaging. I'm excited to use this book to help my family grow, as well as help the families I serve!

> KEVIN L. NICKERSON, founder of GameBreakers
> Academy, NFL chaplain for the Los Angeles Rams

I have known Andy Dooley personally for more than six years now and can attest to the fact that he truly embodies the three foundational pillars that he is so passionate about sharing with the world: faith, family, and fitness. I love the simplicity of his approach, from powerful faith-based lessons to direct calls to action to bring the family closer together!

> CHRIS POWELL, host of ABC's *Extreme*
> *Makeover: Weight Loss Edition*

Far too many parents know they are supposed to be investing in their family's discipleship but feel like it's more of a duty than a joy. Andy Dooley stands in the gap to make real engagement with God's Word both practical and fun. The authenticity and passion I've observed in him as a father comes through in his efforts as an author. Read this book with those you love most—you will not regret it.

> BRIAN MCCORMACK, lead pastor, Reach
> Church, Kirkland, Washington

BUILDING
A FAMILY
OF
FAITH

BUILDING A FAMILY OF FAITH

SIMPLE AND FUN DEVOTIONS TO
DRAW YOU CLOSE TO EACH OTHER
AND NEARER TO GOD

• • •

ANDY DOOLEY

**ZONDERVAN
BOOKS**

ZONDERVAN BOOKS

Building a Family of Faith
Copyright © 2022 by Andy L. Dooley

Requests for information should be addressed to:
Zondervan, *3900 Sparks Dr. SE, Grand Rapids, Michigan 49546*

Zondervan titles may be purchased in bulk for educational, business, fundraising, or sales promotional use. For information, please email SpecialMarkets@Zondervan.com.

ISBN 978-0-310-36615-7 (audio)

Library of Congress Cataloging-in-Publication Data

Names: Dooley, Andy, 1980- author.
Title: Building a family of faith : simple and fun devotions to draw you close to each other and nearer to God / Andy Dooley.
Description: Grand Rapids : Zondervan, 2022. | Summary: "In Building a Family of Faith, leader, pastor, social media influencer, fitness professional, and author Andy Dooley combines Bible stories with engaging physical activities and thoughtful discussion questions to help your family spend quality time together as you learn more about God, faith, and fitness"—Provided by publisher.
Identifiers: LCCN 2022022516 (print) | LCCN 2022022517 (ebook) | ISBN 9780310366126 (trade paperback) | ISBN 9780310366133 (ebook)
Subjects: LCSH: Families—Religious life. | Parenting—Religious aspects—Christianity.
Classification: LCC BV4526.3 .D66 2022 (print) | LCC BV4526.3 (ebook) | DDC 248.8/45—dc23/eng/20220714
LC record available at https://lccn.loc.gov/2022022516
LC ebook record available at https://lccn.loc.gov/2022022517

Cover design: Spencer Fuller / Faceout Studio
Cover illustrations: Shutterstock
Interior design: Denise Froehlich

Printed in the United States of America

22 23 24 25 26 27 28 29 30 /LSC/ 15 14 13 12 11 10 9 8 7 6 5 4 3 2 1

To my beautiful family,
who inspired me to write this—
Tiffany, Hope, Skylee, Andy II, and Ava.
May we stay a close and
loving, fun family of faith.

And to my father, Tom Dooley,
who passed on to heaven
right before I started writing this book.
Thank you for demonstrating
how to be a loving family man.
You now have a new body
and will be forever missed.

CONTENTS

INTRODUCTION

After talking with a lot of people during the COVID-19 pandemic, I realized many families were struggling with connecting and growing together. When everyone was forced to be in close quarters with their loved ones for an extended period of time, many things were exposed in our relationships. I enjoyed having more time with my family, and my heart broke for those who didn't feel the same way—which made me want to create a family-focused, interactive, and fun book with devotions to draw you closer to your family and nearer to God.

You'll have suggested Scriptures to read together. Have fun with those! You can have a family memorizing contest, write the week's verse on a chalkboard or dry-erase board, create artwork based on the verse, take time every day to read and recite the verse, make up a song that uses the verse as lyrics, or get a family treat when everyone has memorized the verse.[1]

Each devotion begins with a "Let's Think about It . . ." section that has some introductory questions the whole family can talk about before continuing with the devotion. Give everyone a chance to answer the questions

---

1. You may find it helpful to also use a kid-friendly Bible translation such as the New International Reader's Version (NIrV) to help your kids better understand the Bible passage for each devotion.

and explain their answers and then launch into the next part, which will be the relatable story, teaching, and learning portion.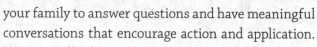

I include a section ("Let's Talk about It . . .") for your family to answer questions and have meaningful conversations that encourage action and application. You can talk about the topic right then, bring it up later in the week, or just encourage family members to think about things on their own. A short family prayer is included near the end. Feel free to use this as a starting point for your own family prayer time. Each devotion closes with a "Let's Act . . ." section that suggests activities you can do together to strengthen what you learned in the devotion. Choose one or two activities to do throughout the week, which can be adapted for a variety of ages. Do what works best for you and your family!

Whether your family has been doing devotions together for years or this is your first time introducing this discipline, I hope *Building a Family of Faith* is just what you need to help your family connect with one another, grow in faith, and learn more about how physical activity can influence your relationships and your faith. I'm a pastor, social media influencer, fitness professional, and father of four who has worked with families for more than eighteen years through sports, fitness, and ministry, and these ideas come from the time I've spent with my own family.

Take the weight off your shoulders and let these devotions help you build a family of faith.

Now go have fun together!

Andy

PRACTICING PATIENCE

Those who hope in the LORD
will renew their strength.
They will soar on wings like eagles;
they will run and not grow weary,
they will walk and not be faint.

Isaiah 40:31

 **? Let's Think about It . . .**

Have you ever had to make a decision that had a limit on it? Maybe it was a money limit. You were at the store, with a certain amount of money to spend, and you saw a ton of things you wanted—clothes, toys, new stuff for your room. You felt like you had to have what you were seeing right there in that moment. How do you feel when you're told you don't have enough money for everything you want and that you'll have to wait until you have more money to buy it all?

What about having to wait for something that you really want to happen? Maybe your family has made plans to go on vacation or on an outing somewhere. Maybe you're planning to have a friend over for a day.

It can be tough to be patient, to have to wait. Waiting is hard. We can even get angry when things don't happen the way we want them to. What emotions do you feel inside when you know you're supposed to be patient but you just don't want to wait, or when things don't turn out the way you hoped they would?

Let's Get into It . . .

Our family loves to visit Target. We joke that they must spray a special scent in the air there—something that puts you in a good mood and keeps you there for hours. The kids get extremely excited whenever we say, "We're going to Target." When we're there, we typically either let them use gift cards they received for their birthdays or holidays or give them a ten-dollar spending limit. If a toy costs $9.99, guess what? They don't have enough (after factoring in tax). We could easily make a rule that says the parents take care of the tax, but we want the kids to learn real-world principles. And if you only have $10, that isn't enough.

Our five-year-old son, Andy II, doesn't understand the concept of money quite yet. He will grab any toy he wants and ask, "Dad, can I have this?" I have to point to the price and say, "Son, this is $49.99. You don't have enough." I never tell him, "You can't have it." I just present him with options. He can either save his money that day or choose a different toy. If he is sleepy or hungry, his lower lip sticks out and his head droops in despair as he walks through the aisles feeling defeated and impatient. But if he has been fed and is feeling awake and happy, I get to watch his little brain process the options. And I can see how he's becoming a bit more understanding of what it means to be patient and have to wait.

My eight-year-old daughter, Hope, has been in these situations quite often. She used to get upset when she couldn't get what she wanted. However, over time she has been learning it's okay to wait and save her money. She can come back later to get what she wants or to find something even better! She's learning the power of patience.

Let's Learn . . .

We are being led by the best, smartest, and strongest of all time. No one has been or ever will be better than God—at being patient *and* at everything else. Because God is the best, we can always tell him exactly how we feel. We can tell him when we feel sad, mad, tired, confused, or even just blah. We can for sure tell him when we feel impatient.

Kids, maybe someone hurt your feelings at school and you just want to tell the whole world about it, right then and there. It can be hard to be patient and just tell God how you feel or wait until you get home and tell your parents what happened. You want to do something about it right now. But God wants you to pray about it and trust him. Sometimes it's better to let your emotions fade a bit so you are more open to receiving good guidance about what to do in the situation. Sometimes you need to wait a little while to help you remember and believe with confidence that God wants only the best for you.

God does not want our emotions to dominate us, and he wants us to include him in every aspect of our lives. We feel lighter and less burdened—and yes, more patient—when God is in control.

No matter how old you are, if you can learn to believe that God wants the best for you and has mapped out your life for good, you will be way ahead in the game of life. That doesn't mean you will get everything you ask for. Things won't always go perfectly or happen just the way you want them to. Just know that if it's not the yes answer or just the timing you wanted, God has something better for you. Be excited if you have to wait because you know something good is coming!

What you want right now may not always be what's best for you. With God, everything is beautiful in its time. God doesn't want what is mediocre or even just okay for you. He wants you to have the very best. If you are willing to be patient, you will be rewarded with the best that God has for you. And it doesn't stop there. When you are willing to learn to be patient, God gives you strength when you feel weak.

God always wants the best for us. Sometimes we just have to wait for it. So trust, be patient, and *wait on God.*

Let's Talk about It . . .

How does being patient make you strong? How does it show that we are trusting God?

Let's Pray . . .

Dear God,
Please guide our family. Guide our decisions. Work on our behalf. Be in our life consistently. Give us the patience to wait and make us strong. Amen.

- Take a trip to Target or another favorite store. Before you go, have each person in the family make a list of things they want to buy. Also, put different amounts of money in different envelopes ($1, $5, $10, $20, and so forth)—one envelope per family member. When you get to the store, each person picks an envelope. The amount in the envelope is the limit you can spend. Purchase your item or items (or you can choose to save the money) and then talk about the experience at home or at dinner or during dessert. What did you hope to buy? What could you actually buy? How hard was this experience?

- Play a game that involves waiting and being patient. You could play a card-matching game indoors or go outside and play "Simon Says." Putting a puzzle together can require a lot of patience. So can learning an advanced game like chess.

- Make a patience jar. Write down some things you really want to do as a family—taking a trip to Disneyland, raising chickens, buying a new TV—but can't afford to do right away. While you're saving money, learn as much as you can about what you're planning to do. This keeps you distracted and busy, and you'll find it much easier to wait.

- Take time to pray together for one another. Pray specifically for each family member's situation and ask for God's strength to embrace patience while that person waits on God and his perfect timing.

2

CREATED TO DO

> My dear brothers and sisters, stand firm. Let nothing move you. Always give yourselves fully to the work of the Lord, because you know that your labor in the Lord is not in vain.
>
> **1 Corinthians 15:58**

Let's Think about It . . .

Do you ever wonder what you were created to do in this world? Do you wonder what your purpose is? A good way to start figuring this out is to pay attention to what you love to do or think of what you're naturally good at. Maybe you can draw well or write interesting stories. Maybe you love to organize and decorate your room. Maybe you're good at running fast or singing or playing an instrument. Maybe you understand math really well, or it's fun and easy for you to make speeches or give presentations. Maybe it's super simple for you to make new friends or get to know your neighbors.

Sometimes as we get older, we may lose sight of our talents because we get so busy with other things. We may have a sudden burst of passion, excitement, or enthusiasm to start a new project or activity. But when things get hard—when we have a setback or wish we could improve faster—we lose motivation. And sometimes we even quit. Has this ever happened to you? Do you wish you had stuck with something or tried a little harder to get to the next level?

Let's Get into It . . .

It's fun to be in discovery mode, recognizing the things that each person in the family is naturally good at and gets excited about. For parents, it's great to pay attention to these talents in the early stages so we can help cultivate our kids' gifts. And for siblings, it's fun to notice what every member does well!

So far our oldest, Hope, loves to create by drawing; engineering cars, planes, and other things out of cardboard; and making bookmarks or creating paper stuffies, as she calls them. She is also a natural athlete who wants to play basketball, gymnastics, track, and soccer and is very competitive. Our second child, Skylee, is a pure performer. She absolutely loves to entertain, sing, dance, and perform. Her current dreams are to do ballet, tap dance, play soccer, and sing. Skylee also has a tender heart and is such an amazing caregiver. Our son, Andy II, thinks he is a superhero and Sonic the Hedgehog. He runs everywhere and says he wants to play basketball. He has a natural athletic ability and seems to be ambidextrous. He has a love for people, cares for others' well-being, and is intelligent. Our daughter Ava is the youngest—not even two yet—but the one thing we do know is that she is a boss. She has a strong personality and thinks she can do everything her siblings can do.

Have fun watching your family evolve in their gifts, and look for ways to support one another along the way.

Let's Learn . . .

Would you say that Jesus is at the center of your family's decisions, thoughts, actions, belief systems, social media, and even dreams? This is important to consider as you figure out what each member of your family was created to do. God's Word should be at the center of everything in your life. If your home base is grounded and centered on Jesus and the Bible, I truly believe each family member will become more likely to continue looking to God as their leader.

Our Bible verse for this devotion, 1 Corinthians 15:58, reminds us to "stand firm" and "let nothing move you" when you are doing the work of God. When we are being led by God, our work will always have a purpose. And that purpose is beyond ourselves. You're not good at math just so you can get 100 percent on your math tests; you're good at math so you can help others. You're not a talented soccer player so you can collect trophies and awards for yourself; your soccer talent can take you places where you can share God's love. Your ability to make friends doesn't just make you popular; it gives you a chance to shine God's light on others. No matter what you're good at, know that God is the one who gave you that gift. And your job is to do your best with it so you can use it for him.

We all play a part in carrying out God's ultimate plan. When you're good at something, people count on you. When God makes you good at something, he intends for you to use that talent to bless others. Your God-given purpose is beyond you. If you let your talents shine for the Lord, you will experience some rewards here on earth, but your greatest rewards will be given in heaven.

You don't have to have everything figured out right now. Some people are still discovering new gifts and talents well into adulthood. And it's not just individuals who have gifts and talents. Families have their own things they're good at, like hosting neighbors for the yearly Christmas party or having a ton of energy to volunteer together at community events. All of us have a purpose, and if God is at the center of our lives, we will live the life God intended us to live.

> God wants us to be diligent in our work for him. Our gifts and talents are not just for ourselves; they are for God and others.

Let's Talk about It . . .

Take a moment and ask each family member, "What are you good at? What do you like to do? What are you passionate about?"

Let's Pray . . .

Dear God,
Thank you for designing each of us so intricately, so specifically, and so unlike anyone else on this planet. Please help us as believers to bring glory to you in everything we do. Amen.

- Spend a week trying new things. Have each family member write down five things they are interested in doing and then do those things. They can be as simple as drawing a picture for someone else or as involved as trying out a new activity, like kids choir or youth sports. At the end of the week, talk about how trying the new things went. Did you have fun? Did someone point out that you had talent? Did the new thing seem like something you would want to keep doing? Can you imagine some ways you could give glory to God and help others by doing these things?

- Make a family plan to volunteer together and share your gifting with others. If your family likes cooking, you can join an organization that helps feed others. If you're super musical, you can lead worship at a church event. If you love sports, you can volunteer at a sporting event or participate in an athletic competition that helps raise money for a good cause.

- Create a family purpose. Brainstorm words you want to put in your purpose. What things are important to your family? What are some characteristics your family has? Is there a Bible verse that is important to your family and that you all want to live by? Write down your family purpose. You can even have someone design artwork—either by hand or digitally—and frame the piece to be displayed in your home.

- Have each member of the family write a "pro and con" list. The list will help everyone figure out their gifting and purpose. Draw a line down the middle of a piece of paper. On the left side of the line at the top, write *PROS*. On the right side of the line at the top, write *CONS*. In the *PROS* section, write out all the things you love doing, things you're good at, or things people have told you you've got talent for. In the *CONS* section, write down the things you don't enjoy doing or feel don't come easily to you. Then look at the list to help figure out what you do best. Your purpose is probably somewhere on that list!

- Look around and notice all the things you're surrounded by—people, animals, art, music, math, athletics, computers, engineering, creating, directing, leading, families, aeronautics, fitness, theology, writing, fashion . . . the list goes on and on. Write down your top ten interests and then seal them in an envelope. Have everyone in the family put their envelopes in a box. A year from now, open the envelopes. Have your top ten interests changed, or have they stayed the same? God is always introducing new things into our lives, but some of our passions stay the same.

3

MEAN WHAT YOU SAY

> Above all, my brothers and sisters, do not swear—not by heaven or by earth or by anything else. All you need to say is a simple "Yes" or "No." Otherwise you will be condemned.
>
> **James 5:12**

Let's Think about It . . .

Do you ever say something you don't mean? Maybe you promise you'll do something, like clean your room or unload the dishwasher, but then you get busy playing a game or watching a show and you don't do what you said you would do. Maybe you ask your parents if you can have something (a snack, help with your homework, a new backpack for school) or do something (watch a show together, have a friend over for a playdate, work on a craft project), and they say, "Sure." But then they get busy and tell you, "I'm sorry. I know I said yes, but it turns out we can't do that today. How about another time?" Or when you ask for

something, they give you that famous two-word answer—
the one you know means *no*: "We'll see"!

I remember my uncle once stated that he would
buy my brother and me a pair of Air Jordans. We
were in utter shock and awe. We even asked, "Are you serious?"
We never requested he do such a thing, yet he randomly pulled us
aside one day and mentioned his idea to us, following it up with
those important words, "I promise." You have to understand that,
at the time, we had never owned a pair of shoes of this magnitude.
Michael Jordan was the G.O.A.T. (Greatest of All Time) in our eyes.

In our neighborhood, anyone who owned a pair of Air
Jordans was like a rainbow-colored, singing unicorn. Owning
these shoes just wasn't common. The only people who could
afford them were wealthy, worked multiple jobs, or were street
hustlers. We didn't know which category our uncle represented,
but we sure weren't going to ask. All we knew is that he was going
to buy us Air Jordans, and we were so excited! My brother and I
kept performing fadeaway jump shots everywhere—around the
house, in the grocery store, at the mall, in Walmart, you name
the place. When we released our imaginary shots, we would yell
out, "JORDAN!" Kids tend not to understand the word *chill* when
they're excited. My brother and I couldn't contain
our excitement. We were far from chill!

Let's Learn . . .

Today's Bible verse, James 5:12, is powerful
because it simplifies the way we Christians
should conduct our speech. As believers in

Jesus, we do not have to convince anyone with a promise, say "I swear," cross our hearts, announce "Scout's honor," or take any other silly oath to prove we will keep our word. Everything we say should be soaked in truthfulness, without any intent to manipulate, deceive, or lie. As the Bible verse says, our yes needs to mean yes, and our no needs to mean no.

Our words need to be truthful and consistent. What people say to one another makes a difference. What you say to your brother or sister has an impact. What parents say to their kids is meaningful. God wants us to say what we mean and mean what we say. Not keeping promises hurts families and makes it hard to trust one another. Ask God to help you be a person whose words can be trusted.

You know the story I told at the beginning of this devotion about my uncle and the Air Jordans? Sadly, my brother and I waited years for him to make good on his promise. But it never happened. I don't believe my uncle meant to be mean to us, but the truth is, our hearts were broken. Our excitement turned to sadness, and we weren't sure we could trust anything our uncle said.

Today I still sometimes struggle when people promise me things or direct impressive words toward me. But I also trust God and choose to believe the best in people. I choose to believe they really do mean what they say, even if they aren't always able to keep their promises. Nobody is perfect, and we'll all make mistakes from time to time. I challenge you to make an intentional effort to invest in the people close to you with your words. Think before you speak. Mean what you say. Let your yes be your yes, and your no be your no.

God wants our words to mean something. He wants us to keep our promises and to be honest when we

say we will do something. We need to always think
before we speak and consider our future actions.

Let's Talk about It . . .

Have you ever promised something you didn't
follow through with and hurt someone else's
feelings? Has someone ever done this to you?
How can you do a better job of saying what
you mean and meaning what you say?

Let's Pray . . .

Dear God,
Please help us with our words—to keep our promises
and mean what we say. Amen.

Let's Act . . .

- Make an "oops jar." Every time someone
  in the family doesn't keep their promise
  or says something they don't mean, they
  have to put a certain amount of money into the jar. (Parents
  can contribute more money than the kids!) At the end of a
  month or even a year, donate the money to a good cause.
- When you want to promise someone something, put it in
  writing! You can write the promises in a notebook or on a
  dry-erase board. When it's in writing, it's harder to break
  a promise. It just seems more *real*. (It also makes you think
  harder about promising someone something if you have to
  write it down!) Here are some examples:

- I *promise we will have a movie night with popcorn and hot chocolate this Friday.*
- I *promise I will fold the laundry today.*
- I *promise we can go to the park the next sunny weekend.*
- Look in the Bible for God's promises. How does God keep his promises? Write down some of God's promises.

4

WHO YOU REP

We are therefore Christ's ambassadors, as though God were making his appeal through us. We implore you on Christ's behalf: Be reconciled to God.

2 Corinthians 5:20

? Let's Think about It . . .

Do you ever feel like you struggle with sharing your faith in Jesus with other people? Is it awkward to talk to non-Christians about Jesus? It can be really hard when you aren't even sure what certain Bible verses or stories mean. Let's face it, there is a lot of tough stuff in the Bible! The good news of the Bible is amazing though. Jesus died on the cross so our sins would be taken away. And Jesus did this because he loves us so, so much. If we decide to let Jesus live in our hearts and be number one in our lives, we will become members of his elite heavenly team forever—and Jesus will help us share the good news with others.

Have you heard the famous saying, "If not us, who? If not now, when?" Those words have stuck with me for a long time. In the world we live in, so many people use these words as a mantra for inspiration to complete a task or to motivate others to get moving and do something. As a Christian family, we like to ask, "If not us, who? If not now, when?" When will we tell others about Jesus and share the good news? And if *we* don't do it, who will?

An *ambassador* is a representative or messenger from one government or country to another. If you are an ambassador, you tell other countries or people about the amazing things that your country has to offer.

When you give your life to God, you become a member of his heavenly team. You become an ambassador of God, and it's your job to share the gospel so that others can know they also can have eternal life. As an ambassador of Christ, you represent your new home—heaven. You have the opportunity to share the good news of Christ with anyone you know. And you're never too young (or too old!) to learn about Jesus and tell your friends all about him and the Bible.

People were created to live together in community. We can help build God's community by sharing the gospel with others. And as God's representatives on earth, it's also our job to spread the wonderful news to people we come in contact with at home, on our sports teams, in the classroom, out on walks with friends, in the neighborhood, at the park or playground, eating in a restaurant, online, and everywhere we go.

Today's Bible verse, 2 Corinthians 5:20, explains how Paul made it his duty to be an ambassador of God sharing about Jesus with people all over who would listen to him or read his letters. Like Paul, we represent someone so cool—someone who brings hope to a dark world, a peace that is beyond amazing, and excitement for an amazing eternal future in heaven.

God's Word is meant to be shared and discussed. Every member of every family can confidently be an ambassador of Christ, representing the gospel everywhere they go and telling others about the incredible things God has to offer.

We were not only created to have a personal relationship with God; we were also created to represent God here on earth.

Let's Talk about It . . .

Can you think of some people who need to hear the good news about Jesus? What are some graceful ways you can share God's love with them?

Let's Pray . . .

Dear God,
Please open up opportunities so we can share your good news with others in ways that are comfortable and natural for us and that they can understand.
Amen.

- Who needs to hear the good news of Jesus? Make a family prayer journal and start praying for everyone you know who you hope will one day join you in heaven. Write down the names of everyone you can think of—from your best friend to your mail carrier to your soccer coach—who needs to hear about God. Think of ways you can reach and share God's love with them in natural and practical ways.

- One of the easiest ways to share Jesus with people is to get to know them. After all, that's what Jesus did! He hung out with people, ate with them, asked them questions, and just spent time with them. So get to know your friends, class-mates, teammates—anyone who's a part of your everyday life. Become actual friends first. Get to know what they like and are interested in. Eat lunch together. Hang out at school. Talk to each other. Have family playdates so everyone can get to know each other. As you become familiar with each other, natural questions will come up, and soon enough you can share about your life, what you do, and what you believe. You can also ask them questions as well. This is a really comfortable, easy way to tell others about why Jesus is such an important part of your life.

- As a family, read through the book of Mark in the Bible. This will give you a fantastic picture of the good news that Jesus came to earth to proclaim.

5

PUSH PAUSE

> By the seventh day God had finished the work he had been doing; so on the seventh day he rested from all his work. Then God blessed the seventh day and made it holy, because on it he rested from all the work of creating that he had done.

Genesis 2:2–3

? Let's Think about It . . .

Do you ever wonder why you have to take a nap or have a bedtime? Wouldn't it be nice if you could skip a nap, stay up all night, or pick your own bedtime? Maybe you feel like there isn't enough time in the day to do everything you want (or need) to do. You know your body needs a rest, but you feel like you have to keep pushing through.

And what about vacation? You circle the date of the vacation on the calendar, plan your trip, pack your things, and get ready to go. The vacation itself is super fun, but when you get back, you're exhausted. In fact, you might feel like you need a vacation from your vacation!

Do you often wake up feeling tired? Do you wish you could have more energy? Or do you feel like you don't need that much sleep and would rather rest less and do more? No matter how you feel, it's important to push pause from time to time.

Let's Get into It . . .

Recently, I found some self-proclaimed fitness gurus online who had created a challenge to do squats and work the legs for thirty days straight with no rest days. Yes, every single day without a miss. I know that for some people, this may not sound like a good idea and sounds like a good way to get hurt. For others, it may sound completely sane. Me? It sounded like a great challenge, so I squatted and worked my legs every day for seven days. On the seventh day, our family was invited to play kickball with some friends. We were super excited to play and compete!

We are a very competitive family, always up for any opportunity to be active. The first round of the kickball game, I stepped up to the plate to kick. I knew everyone assumed I wanted to blow a hole through the ball and kick it out of the park. Instead, I bunted my kick so I could outrun my opponents to each base. I felt great and knew that the next time I was up to kick, I was going to do the complete opposite. My team only scored two points that round, and when we switched to defense, we held the other team to just one point. When it was our team's turn to take the plate and I stepped up again, I knew what strategy I was going to use.

I approached the plate with my game plan to kick the ball into a low-hanging cloud. The pitcher rolled the ball my way, and

I was so focused that it felt like everything had slowed down. As I wound up to kick the ball, I suddenly heard a loud POP! And I felt the vibration throughout my entire body. I knew I had pulled a muscle in my right quadricep / upper leg. And I knew it was bad. My kids rushed over and asked me if I was okay, while my wife was focused on being up next to kick. She may as well have said, "Just put some dirt on it." (Just kidding—kind of.)

I walked off the field and made a phone call to my friends who worked at a cryotherapy clinic, a special kind of medical treatment. That night they were able to see me and from a series of questions diagnosed me with complete muscle fatigue. Training my legs for seven days straight without any rest had a negative impact that resulted in a pulled muscle in my leg.

Let's Learn . . .

There is a time to push hard with school, work, sports, activities, goals, household projects, workouts, dreams, ideas, music, social media—anything you spend time doing. There is also a time to push pause and rest. Look at our Bible verse for today. Even God took time to rest from his work of creating the world.

What we think we can do in seven days God can exceed in the first second of our first day off. If he can do this, just imagine what he can do on our behalf when we choose to honor his commands. But if we don't learn to pause, rest, recover, and remember that everything we have—our lives, our homes, our families, our friendships, our talents, our accomplishments—comes from God, we're not getting it. And we may miss seeing how God is using everything we do to help carry out his big plans for our world.

Pausing to rest and observe the Sabbath allows you to remember who is in charge in your life. You are not the provider; God is. He just wants your unconditional love and your faith in him. When he has those things, he can use you whenever and wherever to help carry out his ultimate plan. Will you choose to be used by God? Or will you try to take his place of leadership? God delivered you all by himself, and he gave you a chance at eternal life. Just imagine what will happen when you trust him with your daily living and obey his commands, including his command to push pause and rest.

God wants us to observe the Sabbath and incorporate regular periods of rest into our busy lives. We need to push pause and reset before we pick things up again.

Let's Talk about It . . .

Does your family observe the Sabbath and take time to rest? If you do, what are some ways you can make your time of rest even more meaningful? If you don't, how can you schedule a family time of rest during the week?

Let's Pray . . .

Dear God,
Thank you for creating seasons in life. Help us to remember there is a time to push and work hard, and a time to push pause and rest. Amen.

- Get out your family calendar. You know, the one that has the million and one activities written on it—basketball games, band concerts, work meetings, vacations, church events. How much white space is on that calendar? How much potential rest time do you see? For the future, block out some family rest time. Maybe it's a whole day. Maybe it's an afternoon or morning once a week. Maybe you need to schedule in an entire weekend of rest. Write down the rest time on the calendar and then stick to your Sabbath.

- Working out is great for you—as long as you take time to rest! Here are two fun options for weeklong workouts. You can modify the workouts for younger or less active family members. Do half of the workout, break up the exercises throughout the day, or even skip a few of the harder exercises. But make sure you start somewhere! When you've worked hard, your well-earned rest time is such a great reward.[1]

WORKOUT #1

- Day 1: 100 air squats
- Day 2: walk 10,000 steps
- Day 3: 50 push-ups
- Day 4: 100 ab mat sit-ups
- Day 5: 2 minutes of burpees (as many as you can do)
- Day 6: 3 sets of cat/cow stretches
- Day 7: rest/pause

---

1. For guidance on some of these exercises, you can find various videos on my YouTube channel (www.youtube.com/c/AndyDooleyFitness/videos).

WORKOUT #2

- Day 1: 50 air squats
- Day 2: walk 5,000 steps
- Day 3: 25 push-ups
- Day 4: 50 ab mat sit-ups
- Day 5: hand planks for 30 seconds
- Day 6: 3 sets of 6 pop squats
- Day 7: rest/pause

- Set up a family rest area in your house. It could include pillows and blankets, fun books, a place to put a water bottle or a cup of tea or hot chocolate. When someone is feeling overwhelmed, they can push pause and head for the family rest area to recharge.

6

UNDERSTANDING THE BIBLE

> Your word is a lamp for my feet,
> a light on my path.
>
> **Psalm 119:105**

? Let's Think about It . . .

I believe that learning to study your Bible is about the most exciting thing you could ever do. But a lot of people don't really know how to study the Bible. They aren't even sure how to get started. Should you read the Bible like a regular book, from front to back? Should you underline or highlight in your Bible? And what about this journaling thing that seems to be really popular? Should that be a part of your Bible study?

Let's Get into It . . .

Most people struggle to understand the Bible when they read it. There are a lot of good reasons for this. The Bible was written a long time ago, so the people and places and events seem kind of strange. It was a different culture back then. The language was different. And a lot has happened historically since the Bible was written. I personally struggled with Bible reading early on, mostly because I didn't understand the style of writing in the King James Version translation. I was young and could not relate. I also didn't understand how to study my Bible in a way that would help me get to know God. In Bible study or youth group, the teacher would explain the stories, which helped, but they weren't with me every time I read my Bible, which discouraged me. When I learned how to invite God into my reading time, everything changed for me.

Let's Learn . . .

The main reason we should want to read our Bibles is that the Bible is God's Word. It's like a personal letter or text message to us about the past and how it applies to right now and the future. Life can get hard at times, especially as we get older and have more responsibilities and experience more things. We all need the direction of God's Word when we're figuring out how to get through tricky situations or make hard decisions. When we read the Bible and learn about Jesus, we learn to see things the way Jesus sees them. The Bible gives us hope and power to defeat the lies and temptations of this world.

There is something amazing about reading and studying God's Word on our own as we sit down with our Bible (which could be an actual book or a phone app or even an audiobook version of the Bible), study tools (pens or pencils, a notebook or journal), and the Holy Spirit. And after we spend time alone with God, studying his Word, we are able to understand the Bible better. This means we will be able to talk with other believers about

God. Reading and falling in love with the Bible is the foundation for change in us and in others. Studying God's Word will give us the tools we need to live our lives the way Jesus wants us to.

Imagine going on a family walk at night. It would be scary if you failed to bring a light to see where you were going. But if you brought a flashlight or headlamp or used the light on your phone, you could see what was in front of you. That light could save you from stepping on dog poop, slipping on ice, tripping over the uneven sidewalk, and so many other things that could harm you.

God's Word protects us in the same way. The Bible's teaching is like a flashlight to our feet in the dark. It helps us navigate our way through life and avoid the things that can trip us up. We need God's Word in our lives daily. If we commit to reading our Bibles and learning more about the Lord, the hunger and desire to know him better will grow.

And when you read your Bible, don't just read it to read it. Read it to understand and apply it to your everyday life.

God wants us to not just read the Bible. He also wants us to study his Word and apply it to our lives in a practical way. We are to think deeply about what he says and store his words in our hearts.

Let's Talk about It . . .

What is it about the Bible that confuses you the most? What do you want to understand better? What does it mean to apply what we learn in the Bible to our daily lives?

Dear God,
Thank you for giving us your Word—the Bible. Help
us not only to read our Bibles but also to put your
words into action so they can change our lives and
the lives of others. Amen.

Let's Act . . .

- Go for a family night walk. Bring a source of lighting—a flashlight, a headlamp, a phone light—but spend some of the time trying to walk without the light. When you get home, talk about walking in the light versus walking in the darkness. What happened? How did you feel? Which do you think is the best way to walk—with or without the light?

- Read a portion of the Scriptures and then watch a televised version on that part of the Bible to help bring God's Word to life. Check out YouTube, Amazon Prime Video, Netflix, Hulu, or any other online video streaming sources to find a good version. I recommend The Bible Project (www.bible-project.com) and RightNow Media (www.rightnowmedia.org) as great resources to check out.

- Choose a weekly verse for your family to practice saying and memorizing throughout the week. At the end of the week, select a time for everyone in the family to recite the verse. (Younger kids could draw a picture or say a few key words from the verse.) If you recite the verse word for word, you win a prize. Or if the entire family nails the verse, you all go out for dinner or dessert or do something fun together.

- Find a Bible version that everyone in your family likes and can understand. A few we really like that work well for most ages are *The Message* paraphrase, the New Living Translation, and the Contemporary English Version. The New International Version and the English Standard Version are great version for adults. When you're studying the Bible, take your time and read it slowly. Don't rush through the words. Read out loud if it helps you retain the information better. Then ask lots of questions, such as, *Who is this about? What is happening? Where does it take place? When in history did this happen? What else is going on?*
- When you're reading the Bible and trying to get all you can out of it, remember this helpful acrostic (STUDY):

  Study
  Take your time
  Understand
  Decide to apply
  You need to pray

- Add another element to your Bible study. Reading God's Word is great, but you can add something else to help you understand and apply it better. Write down your own personal thoughts and ideas in a journal after you've read the passage together as a family. You might choose an arts and crafts project revolving around what you read. Or you might act out the Bible story, complete with costumes, to really bring it to life.

7

LOSE THE PRIDE

When pride comes, then comes disgrace,
but with humility comes wisdom.

Proverbs 11:2

? Let's Think about It . . .

Do you sometimes find it hard being told what to do or what not to do? Do you get upset when someone corrects you or gives constructive criticism? Do you get defensive when someone says you're wrong or points out something you did wrong? Do you feel like you always need to win an argument? Is it hard for you to say I'm sorry and apologize? Is it hard for you not to interrupt others when they are speaking? When you do something well—like do a good job helping out around the house, get great grades on tests, or win an award—do you need a lot of attention for that? Do you like to always be the center of attention? In short, do you have issues with pride?

Let's Get into It . . .

Pride is at the root of sin. Pride is basically thinking we are better than others. And when we feel this way, it affects how we treat others. Pride is poison to our family relationships and friendships. Pride is horrible and awful and will really mess up our lives if it isn't stopped and corrected by God's work in us to create a heart of humility.

God does not like a prideful person. God hates pride. Proverbs 8:13 says, "To fear the LORD is to hate evil; I hate pride and arrogance." The Bible speaks strongly against pride! That's because pride can really ruin our relationship with God. Pride is about exalting ourselves instead of exalting him. Pride will push us away from God and bring us pain, loneliness, sadness, and nothing good. And that's why we should turn away from being proud and instead work to be the opposite of proud, which is *humble*.

Let's Learn . . .

Pride does not lead to kindness. Today's Bible verse says that when pride comes, disgrace follows. The fruit of pride is rotten fruit, and it affects your interactions with everyone around you. Also, God opposes the prideful, which means he fights against those who are full of pride and arrogance. I can tell you right now, you don't want God fighting against you or your family. You will not win. Ever.

Trading pride for humility can open us up to receiving God's wisdom and help us find joy in serving others. The Bible tells us that Jesus himself was a perfect example of humility. The apostle Paul writes that Jesus "made himself nothing," even though he had all the glory, and he "humbled himself by becoming obedient to death—even death on a cross!" (Philippians 2:7–8) to open for us the way to eternal life.

Because Jesus lived a life of humility, it should be our daily mission to live lives of humility. The reason we should desire to live a life of humility is that God hates pride. Pride is sin. As Christians, we should love the things God loves and hate the things he hates.

When we wake up, God should be at the center of our waking. God should be at the center of how we treat other people. God should be at the center of our thoughts throughout the day. Before we react to any situation or any person, God should be our filter, and we should ask him to help us know how to respond. We should make sure God is at the center of everything in our life—our decisions, our wins and losses, our successes and failures, our relationships with our family and friends and anyone else we spend time with, the way we talk to and interact with other people. In a word, *everything*. To live a life of humility, we need to take the spotlight off ourselves and make God the center of everything in our lives.

> God wants us to be humble. Being humble
> is the opposite of being proud, and all
> sins are rooted in pride. If we are humble,
> God gets the attention and the glory.

Let's Talk about It . . .

What can you do to get rid of your pride and stop making yourself the center of everything? How can you as a family work toward becoming humble followers of Jesus and putting the Lord in the spotlight?

Let's Pray . . .

Dear God,
We want to live a life that is pleasing to you. We do not want to be just hearers of your life-giving message; we also want to be doers. If pride exists within us, either individually or as a family, please forgive us. We repent. We want to live a life of humility. Point out the pride in us so we can get rid of it, and please give us humility so we can be used by you. Amen.

Let's Act . . .

- Look up some of the verses in the Bible that mention either *pride* or *humility*. Write down a few verses that stand out. What does God say about pride? What does God say about humility? Start looking for these qualities in others—people you know, famous people, even characters in books and movies—and notice how their lives are affected by being either proud or humble.

- Look up some famous quotes about being humble and not being proud. Find one that your family likes a lot and create some artwork that you can display in your home.

- Go to a sporting event or watch an athletic competition on television. Notice how the competitors act. Are they proud? Are they humble? Do they seem like good teammates? Being humble doesn't mean you don't play hard or aren't an intense competitor. But watch the way the competitors interact with their teammates or their opponents. Whom do you admire? How would you want to be like them?

8

SEND US

Then I heard the voice of the Lord saying, "Whom shall I send? And who will go for us?"
And I said, "Here am I. Send me!"

Isaiah 6:8

? Let's Think about It . . .

Do you know what it means to be used by God? If not, that's okay. Just know that you were created by God to help fulfill a huge plan. And once you realize this, you can start thinking about having a heart that is willing to be used by God. What if God asked you and your family to drop everything and do something different—move to another city or state or even another country, have the kids change schools, have the parents change jobs, sell your house and move to another location? Could you completely submit to God by saying *yes*?

Maybe you don't feel like you're good enough or important enough to be used by God. You compare yourself to others and think, *I'm not as good as they are.* Or maybe doing your own thing sounds like more fun. Doing what God wants you to do sounds too hard, so you'll let him use someone else. But he doesn't want you to only spend time with him during family devotional time, at Sunday school, or when you're reading the Bible or praying. He wants you to be available all the time. He wants to work through you, as you use your special talents to help the people around you. More than anything, he wants you to be available.

Let's Get into It . . .

It was a sunny Friday afternoon in Ventura, California. I had just finished my gym session at our local LA Fitness, and it was time for my protein smoothie. As I darted out of the gym and jumped into my car, I could already taste the smoothie—I was that hungry! As I started to exit the parking spot, a car pulled out in front of me, forcing me to slam on my brakes. At that moment I could feel the sweat start to bead up on my nose. I was upset! Why couldn't she have waited for me to pull out first?

Because I was mad, I sped up and drove extremely close to this woman's bumper as I followed her out of the parking lot. I was even plotting how I could pull around her at just the right moment. However, she chose to keep angering me by driving slowly. When I tried to pass her, she would speed up. At this point, I had forgotten my smoothie. I just wanted to follow her and make her as mad as she had made me! Now, I know I was being totally immature. But ego and pride had set in, and I was red-hot and upset. She made a left; I made a left. She entered the freeway; I entered the freeway. She sped up; I sped up. She changed lanes; I changed lanes.

Through my anger, I felt in my spirit God telling me to stop.

He was telling me my behavior did not represent his heart. Everything in me wanted to ignore God and keep trying to get back at the woman who had pulled out in front of me. But I finally woke up and came to my senses. I knew that if I wanted to be used by God, I had to submit to his authority.

And when he told me to stop, I needed to stop, because there was a bigger picture than this moment. God could have been looking out for my safety. I could have gotten into a bad accident or been pulled over by the police. I would have looked like a bad representative for Christ if this woman had seen me and then showed up at my church. I would have been forever known as the road-raging, car-chasing jerk who claimed to be a Christian.

Let's Learn . . .

We all have choices in our lives. There are times when our human nature wants to lead and call the shots, which will only create roadblocks and lead to self-centeredness and pride. When we act out of a spirit of selfishness, we are more prone to resist God's call to be available to him.

By the same token, when we second-guess our worth and don't live our lives asking God to use us for his plans and his purposes, we forget we are royalty and joint heirs with Christ. It's easy to compare ourselves to others and see their talents as better than ours. When we do this, we refuse to be used. But our goal is to be like Isaiah in today's Bible verse. Isaiah heard a voice from the Lord asking, "Whom shall I send? Who is willing to be used by me at any time and in any way needed?" Instead of making excuses or looking around for God to pick someone else, Isaiah said, "Here am I. Send me!" Isaiah's response was a heart decision to be used by God. He had a desire to obey and to say yes to whatever God asked him to do.

I challenge you as a family to keep spending time with God and with one another. The more you grow together in God, the more you will stoke the flame to be used by him. God doesn't need you to accomplish his purposes. He can do that on his own. But he wants to work alongside you and bless you. He wants to see you live a fulfilling life, a life you were created to live.

Imagine families all over the world, submitting to God with humble hearts just like Isaiah. Kids, imagine the change and impact you can have on your friends and classmates. Parents, imagine how you can influence others for good—at work, in your neighborhood, wherever you meet people. Telling God, "Yes, use me," will bring an unexplainable joy to your heart, to God's heart, and to the world around you.

> Growing in God ignites a desire to be used
> by him. Make yourself available to God. Tell
> him you're up for whatever plan he has for you.
> Respond to him by saying, "I'm here. Send me!"

Let's Talk about It . . .

Do you want to be used by God? If not, why not? Talk about the reasons you may or may not want to be used by God, and spend time encouraging one another that God can use every single family member to help fulfill his plan.

Dear God,
Please show us what our family can specifically do
to bless others while we are together on this earth.
Help us to always be ready to be used by you to do
good. Amen.

Let's Act . . .

- Make a list of all the ways your family can imagine God using you for good in the community. Then create a family plan for helping others.
- Play a cooperative board game where the players help each other instead of competing against each other. These games may be hard at first if you love to compete, but you'll soon discover that working together can also be fun as you "compete" against a situation. In fact, you may discover you prefer this kind of game! (You can also visit an escape room to have the same type of cooperative experience.)
- Look in the Bible for people who did crazy hard things in God's name. (For instance, would *you* choose to have God send you into a lions' den?) Learn more about these heroes of the Bible and how God did amazing things when they told him, "Send me!" You can even write your own stories about their adventures or act them out.

⇒ 9 ⇐

FORGIVENESS

"When you stand praying, if you hold anything against anyone, forgive them, so that your Father in heaven may forgive you your sins."

Mark 11:25

Let's Think about It . . .

Is forgiveness tough for you? If so, you are in good company. Forgiveness is hard for everyone! No one likes to feel like they are the weaker person, and apologizing isn't easy. It takes a lot of work to forgive someone who hurt you or made you feel sad. Sometimes the pain, anger, embarrassment, and stress that go along with forgiveness can be overwhelming. In most cases, other people would completely understand why you are upset and don't want to forgive. But as hard as forgiveness is, unforgiveness is even worse.

Let's Get into It . . .

Did you know that forgiveness is actually impossible for us to do on our own? Trying to forgive in our own strength is too much for us. We can't do it. That's why we need the supernatural power from the Lord to give us the grace to forgive. It has been said that not forgiving someone is like drinking poison yourself and then waiting for the other person to die. Unforgiveness can be very harmful to people. It can create actual health problems like anxiety, sleeplessness, and depression.

Let's Learn . . .

Forgiveness comes from God. We need his power in order to forgive others. We might think we are being strong by holding our ground and refusing to forgive someone else, but actually we're being weak. Unforgiveness comes from the depths of weakness.

Don't let unforgiveness ruin your life. We sin and hurt God's feelings every single day, multiple times a day. And we expect that God will forgive us. However, God makes it very clear in multiple Scriptures that if you don't forgive others for their wrongdoing, your Father in heaven will not forgive you. That's why we should always ask for God's strength to forgive and why we should always want to be forgiven for our sins and mistakes. It's not worth letting someone else wreck your life because you refused to ask God to help you forgive them.

People can be rude, mean, unfair, hurtful, or downright nasty. Kids can definitely be this way! It doesn't feel good when people make fun of you, call you names, exclude you from a group of friends, and make you feel lonely. But know that Jesus understands this. When he was here on earth, some people were really mean to him. Yes, he definitely understands.

God wants you to know that in forgiveness, there is power, blessing, and a new beginning. When someone hurts you, pay attention to how you feel. Talk to someone you trust. Pray to God about the emotions racing through you. Then make the decision to ask God to give you the grace to forgive those who have hurt you.

Forgiveness is a choice, and once we forgive, we must let it go. When we forgive, it doesn't mean we give in and say that what the other person did was right. That's not our concern because it's not in our hands to right the wrong. That's God's job. Instead, when we forgive, we open the door to allow the Creator of the universe to work on our behalf. It's freeing to know the battle is not ours to fight; the battle is the Lord's. So be forgiving and be free.

God wants us to be forgiving. He wants us to let go of the anger, hurt, sadness, and frustration we experience when we aren't willing to forgive someone else. And he wants us to experience the joy of forgiveness.

Let's Talk about It . . .

Why is forgiveness a good thing? Is there anyone in your life you need to forgive? If you can't think of anyone right away, ask God to bring that person into your mind so you can work on forgiving them.

Let's Pray . . .

Dear God,
Forgiveness is hard! But because you are good and forgive us, we need to forgive others. Help us to see that there is strength in forgiveness and that freedom comes when we choose to forgive others. Amen.

- Make a forgiveness jar. Anytime someone does something or says something
  mean to you, write down what they did or said
  on a piece of paper and put it in the jar. Then spend time
  asking God to help you forgive. When the jar starts to get
  full, take out the papers and burn them in the fireplace or
  outside in a firepit, or tear them up and toss them in the
  recycling bin. Remember that you are forgiven by God,
  and he gives you the strength to forgive others.

- Did you know there are ways to say "I'm sorry" besides
  using your words? Of course, it's good to ask for forgiveness in the traditional way: "I'm sorry. Will you forgive
  me?" But you can also show you're sorry through your
  actions. Bake your best friend some cupcakes to accom-
  pany your apology for having said mean things to her.
  Help your parents with yardwork to demonstrate that
  you're sorry for not doing your chores and talking back.
  Parents, take your kids on a special weekend trip to say
  you're sorry for yelling at them while you were having a
  stressful day. There are so many ways you can demonstrate through your actions that you're sorry.

- Learn to say "I'm sorry" in another language. In every culture, in every part of the world, asking for forgiveness is
  an important part of getting along with others.

10

HOW TO PRAY

When you pray, do not be like the hypocrites, for they love to pray standing in the synagogues and on the street corners to be seen by others. Truly I tell you, they have received their reward in full. But when you pray, go into your room, close the door and pray to your Father, who is unseen. Then your Father, who sees what is done in secret, will reward you. And when you pray, do not keep on babbling like pagans, for they think they will be heard because of their many words. Do not be like them, for your Father knows what you need before you ask him.

Matthew 6:5–8

Let's Think about It . . .

Have you ever wondered about the right way to pray? Is it hard to stop everything and just pray? Do you hear other people say impressive prayers with all the right words and think to yourself, *I could never do that*? Do you skip praying out loud and say, "Pass," because you think you'll say the wrong thing or sound stupid? Believe it or not, every one of us feels this way at times!

Let's Get into It . . .

Even though I grew up with parents who were pastors, they still had to teach their kids how to pray from a sincere heart and how to pray continuously. Prayer didn't just naturally happen for us kids because our parents were in ministry! I'll never forget how I felt when I joined a new church right after college and heard the people in the church praying. It was so different from what I had known growing up! Immediately, I felt insecure and inadequate—as if I had no clue how to actually pray—even though I had grown up around prayer my entire life. It was a terrible feeling. I didn't want to pray out loud because I thought I would be judged for the way I spoke to God. And unfortunately, some of those people may have used fancy words that sounded religious, but in reality, they were not living very godly lives.

Let's Learn . . .

Nobody is perfect. All of us are continually learning and growing. However, God makes it clear in the Bible that he cares about our hearts and our intentions when we pray. He does not care about how beautiful and bold our prayers are. He does not care how many big, biblical words we use in our prayers.

Before our family made a big move across the country, I did my research on apartments and homes in the Pacific Northwest via a VR (virtual reality) headset. I love technology—I can't help it—and through technology, I was able to see inside homes and look around them while living in a different state. It was so cool. However, as real as it appeared, it was still not the real thing. It was *virtual* reality—a place that wasn't real on the inside but simply appeared to be.

Some people who pray, like a VR headset, are projecting something on the outside—all the right words, the image of being a perfect Christian—that isn't really who they are on the inside. They pray to gain public praise and applause from people. And that will be the extent of their reward. But we shouldn't want praise and applause from others. We should want to have eternal rewards from our heavenly Father, as we pray quietly and sincerely. Now this doesn't mean we should never pray out loud or publicly. It just means that when we do pray publicly, it's important to pray from a heart that is God-centered instead of worrying about what other people think of our prayers.

When you pray, take your time and think about God. Think about how awesome he is and how much he loves you. Don't worry about what anyone else thinks of your prayer. (After all, you're not praying for them!) As you grow in Christ, you will grow in your prayer life as well. Read today's Bible passage to remind yourself that you don't need to impress anyone when you pray. You just need to take time to talk to God and build a relationship with him. This will bring you peace and confidence as you pray.

Read the Lord's Prayer in Matthew 6:9–14 to learn how Jesus wants us to pray. When you pray, make sure you're thinking about things that will last forever and things that are important to God. As Christians, we pray to a God whose kingdom is not of this world. Prayer is a gift and a tool for communicating with the Creator of our world. God wants to communicate with us, and we should want to communicate with him.

God wants us to spend time with him in prayer. He cares more about the act of praying than the kind of prayer we say. Talk to God like you would talk to your best friend.

Let's Talk about It . . .

How has your perspective on prayer changed after learning more about talking to God? What are some things you can do to make prayer an everyday part of your life?

Let's Pray . . .

Dear God,
Thank you for giving us the gift of prayer so we can communicate with you. Please help us to remember that even when we don't have all the right words or know exactly what we want to say, you still want to hear from us. Amen.

Let's Act . . .

- While there is no specific right or wrong way to pray, you can learn to become a better pray-er. When you pray, practice doing these things:

  1. Begin your prayer by addressing God. After all, he is the one you are talking to.
  2. Show gratitude when you pray. Praise God for who he is and tell him what you are thankful for. Thank him during the good times and also during the bad times.

3. Share your heart, thoughts, desires, and concerns. Ask God for his supernatural strength to help you through any challenges you are facing.
4. Ask God for forgiveness. Unforgiveness in your heart will block God's forgiveness toward you. Also ask for protection from Satan's attempts to distract you from what God has planned for you.
5. Believe that God wants to work alongside you. Trust that he has your best interests at heart.
6. Close your prayer in the name of Jesus and with an amen. He is our Savior, and when you say "amen," you are agreeing with what was said in the prayer.

- Read some prayers from the Bible. The book of Psalms is full of prayers you can pray when you are feeling happy, sad, anxious, afraid, angry, worried, or confused. Psalms seems to have a prayer for every emotion! See Psalms 3–7, 23, 27, 34, 37, 46, 56, 109, and 143 for examples, among so many others.
- Make a prayer journal. Write down your prayers, as well as when and how God answers them. It's such a great feeling to look back and be able to see how God has been at work in your life.

11

CHOOSE JOY

A cheerful heart is good medicine, but a crushed spirit dries up the bones.

Proverbs 17:22

Let's Think about It . . .

How do you look at life? Are you a cup-half-full or a cup-half-empty type of person? Are you more of a positive person or a negative person? Do you tend to look for the good in people, or does the bad stand out? Would you say you feel happy most of the time, or do you often feel sad? Do you like to laugh and have fun, or do you think life is more serious? Are you a light to your family and friends, or do you tend to cast a shadow around you?

Let's Get into It . . .

I enjoy spending time on social media and creating content. It truly is a creative outlet and brings me joy to know that my content can bring about positive emotions in people all over the world. However, the opposite is also true. There are times when I stumble across an account, and the majority of the content is depressing and dark, which causes my heart to break for that person. I can physically feel my mood start to change, and I have to make a deliberate choice to find another site or content creator to look at and choose joy.

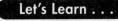

Let's Learn . . .

The wisdom in today's Bible verse says that a joyful heart is good medicine. Joy and laughter play an important part in our lives. God created us to make a choice to embrace joy. In fact, the Bible has a lot to say about the importance of joy. Joy is a direct result of learning about, spending time with, and experiencing the goodness of Jesus. Joy is all about fully trusting the Lord and relying on him to make your heart full of peace.

Heavenly kingdom joy is different from the way the world views joy. Kingdom joy comes from the Lord, and its only source is God. It's awesome to receive presents and to enjoy the finer things of life on earth, but that's not where true joy comes from. Every one of us will experience tough times, pain, disappointment, sadness, confusion, and other negative emotions. We may lose friendships, struggle with a disability or an illness, or just plain have bad days when nothing seems to go our way.

Without Jesus in our lives, we can easily fail to choose joy and instead let a broken spirit take over our lives. Wallowing in sadness and despair may even feel good and right in the moment. But in the long run, negativity will break us down and ultimately destroy us. It is not a fun way to live, and it is not the way God intended us to live.

Choose what God wants for you. Choose a life of joy. Smile more. Laugh more. Look for the little things—a pretty sunset, your playful kitten, a freshly baked chocolate chip cookie—and appreciate them. Joy is infectious, which means it spreads to other people. Your joy can become their joy, which can become someone else's joy. Pretty soon, there's a whole lot of joy out there!

Add joy to your everyday life, whether it's at school, at work, at home, with friends, on vacation, on a sports team, with your family, or even alone with Jesus. Give praise to God. Speak kind words to people. Be loving and grateful. Practicing joy can act like a spiritual massage for your body. It relaxes you, heals you, and brings you peace. Choose a life of joy.

God wants all of us to live a life of joy. This doesn't mean things will always be perfect, but it does mean we need to do our best to see things through his eyes and appreciate everything he has given us.

Let's Talk about It . . .

What is your natural response when things don't go your way? Do you shake it off and try to look on the bright side, or does the complaining start? What can you do to resist having a bad attitude and start choosing joy?

Let's Pray . . .

Dear God,
Thank you for giving us the gift of joy. We know that life isn't always easy. That's why we need you to be the center of every part of our lives, bringing us strength when we are weak, and joy when we are feeling down. Help us to open our hearts to your joy and then pass that joy on to others. Amen.

- Did you know it's almost impossible for someone to not smile back at someone who has a smile on their face? Try it! Smile at someone right now and see how long it takes for them to smile back. (While I was writing this, I looked at my wife in the living room and just called her name while smiling at her. When she looked at me, she immediately started smiling and said, "What?") You can play the smile game anytime you want to bring more happiness into your world.

- Go around the room with everyone in your family and take turns saying what you . . .

  > . . . like about each one of your family members;
  >
  > . . . love about each one of your family members; and
  >
  > . . . think is really cool about each of your family members (a.k.a. giving a compliment).

- Find some praise songs that have the word *joy* in them. Listen to these songs when you're feeling like you need some of God's joy in your life. Your family can even make a "joy" playlist to listen to at home or when you're in the car.

⇒12⇐

YOU BETTER BELIEVE IT

The angel answered, "The Holy Spirit will come on you, and the power of the Most High will overshadow you . . . For no word from God will ever fail."

"I am the Lord's servant," Mary answered. "May your word to me be fulfilled." Then the angel left her.

Luke 1:35–38

? Let's Think about It . . .

How do you feel when you hear someone say, "Nothing is impossible with God"? Do you agree with that statement, or do you immediately think of things that could never be possible? Do you have dreams you want to come true? What are some of those dreams? Do they seem possible? Are you willing to trust God and believe he can help you achieve your dreams?

Do you know how many times I've been told I don't fit in somewhere? Countless times I was told, "You don't fit in this organization [or job, friend group, town, or state]." No, I'm not exaggerating. I was told this because I was different and refused to be like anyone else. In fifth grade, I told my parents and some friends that I would receive an NCAA Division 1 full-ride scholarship in football and most of my peers doubted me and told me it would never happen because I went to a small high school.

I was raised by my parents to live a life of outlandish faith. I was taught that nothing is too big for God. The fact that other people cannot relate to your dreams doesn't mean they will not come to pass. Despite those who think there is a limit to God, I didn't and don't. I received a full-ride football scholarship to Miami of Ohio, and in that moment it increased my faith to trust God and believe that the impossible could be possible and that if it doesn't come to pass, it's because God intended it to be that way, which is a win.

Let's Learn . . .

If you are on God's team, you have already won. There isn't anything that is too big or too hard for God. In this world, Satan will try to distract, derail, and defeat you. However, Jesus was sent to earth with a purpose. He endured all of Satan's temptations and then made the ultimate sacrifice for us. He passed every single test this world threw at him, and then he died on a cross to give us eternal life. It was pretty intense, but Jesus had already won.

Before Jesus was born on earth, God made sure to let the serpent, who was used by Satan in the Garden of Eden, know that he was doomed. (You can read about it in Genesis 3.) God told how Jesus our Savior would come to fatally crush Satan's head and that Satan would only barely bruise the heel of the Savior. This happened, of course, when people turned on Jesus and cried out for him to be crucified on the cross. But he only stayed in the grave for three days before he rose from the dead. Jesus' death ended Satan's rule over us.

A major player in this story was Mary, the mother of Jesus. An angel appeared to her and asked her to do the impossible. Mary was just a humble, lowly servant of God. But she had made God number one in her life, and she trusted him to do big things. When she heard the news that she, a virgin, was going to have a baby, she simply said, "May your word to me be fulfilled." God said it, and she believed it.

I pray that all of us have Mary's attitude toward God's involvement in our lives. Some of us have our own plans and ideas about how things should work out or come to pass. But God's plans and ideas are always much better than our own. I challenge you to leave room for God to do more than your plans, rearrange your dreams, show you his "impossible" ideas (which, of course, *are* possible because he's God), and do amazing things in your life.

There is nothing too big for our God! We tend to dream too small. The way to dream big is to put God at the center of your dreams and then give your intentions, plans, and desires to him so he can guide you into the future. As a family with God at the center, you possess limitless possibilities to impact this planet!

God wants us to know that nothing is too big for him. When we allow him to work in our lives, he is able to use us in the best way for us and the best way for him.

Can you think of a situation where it seemed impossible for you to do something to fix things—or that something good would come out of it? How did you handle the situation? Knowing that nothing is impossible for God, what would you do differently if you were in the same situation again?

Let's Pray . . .

Dear God,
Thank you for your work in our family's life. Nothing is too big for you, and nothing is impossible for you! Help us to truly believe this and to trust you in all things. Amen.

Let's Act . . .

- Spread a big sheet of paper on the table and have everyone in the family write down everything they could ever dream of doing or being in life. What do the kids want to do when they grow up? What new things do the parents want to start doing? Think of jobs, hobbies, activities, ideas, plans and anything else you can imagine. Dream big! Then pray that God will help you accomplish the things he wants you to accomplish.

- Dreams don't come true without hard work! While God may support your dream, he will not just hand it to you on a silver platter. If you dream of becoming a better athlete, make a practice chart and put in the work. The same goes for your dream of getting really good at music or writing or anything else. Pray, put in the work, and allow God to help you grow. Remember, nothing is impossible with God!

SELF-CONTROL

The fruit of the Spirit is love, joy, peace, forbearance, kindness, goodness, faithfulness, gentleness and self-control. Against such things there is no law.

Galatians 5:22–23

Let's Think about It . . .

How often do you struggle to keep your cool? Are you often impatient? Do you tend to get upset if you can't figure something out? Maybe you struggle to take a toy out of the package, tie your shoe, or figure out a word in a book. Do you ever get upset with a brother or sister or friend because they won't share with you or play a game right? How do you keep yourself calm and not fall apart when your LEGO creation gets knocked over? Do you get annoyed if you can't get the attention of someone (like a parent or teacher) when you have something important to say? What about parents? Does stress affect the way you treat your family, friends, and coworkers? When the world feels out of control, how are we expected to control ourselves?

As a kid, if I lost something or forgot anything, I would turn into a human tornado and destroy anything in my path. If I lost a toy, I would throw things around and cry because I was so mad. Here's a good example of what I was like. Have you ever seen magic candles? They are candles that when you blow them out, they relight. Imagine trying to blow out candles on a birthday cake and having everyone watch you as you attempt to blow them out over and over. When I had magic candles on the cake at my birthday party, I would get so frustrated, angry, impatient, and embarrassed that I would start to cry as I tried again and again to blow them out.

Let's Learn . . .

Just because you have become a Christian doesn't mean you will magically master self-control. It takes time and an understanding of who Jesus is and how the Holy Spirit lives in you to improve in this area. As you get to know Jesus better, you see more and more how he exercised self-control when he was on earth. For example, he was a master at *responding* instead of *reacting*. When we react to something or someone, we let our emotions take the wheel and be in control of our words and actions. But when we respond, we take time think about the situation, assess it, reason with ourselves (and maybe others), and receive direction from the Holy Spirit about what to do.

Reacting and responding can often look identical but feel completely different. For example, let's say Mom is at work and her boss treats her unfairly and upsets her. If her reaction is to yell out to her boss, "I quit!"—because her emotions are high and she feels humiliated and doesn't want to be in that environment any longer—that feels quite different than responding to her boss with a request to meet together and then saying, "After careful thought and prayer, I want to put in my two weeks' notice and resign." Same destination, different path to getting there. It always works better when our emotions don't control the situation.

As Christians, self-control is one of the most important fruit of the Spirit we can possess. Self-control keeps us out of trouble, results in good relationships, opens doors to success, helps us become more like Christ, and can even save our lives. Within a family, self-control leads to a better understanding of one another, more love in the household, increased joy and peace in the home, more patience with each other, and togetherness in living for Jesus.

When a situation triggers you to react, think of Proverbs 14:29: "Whoever is patient has great understanding, but one who is quick-tempered displays folly." If you show great understanding, that means you are responding. If you pop off with a quick temper without thinking, that reaction will probably have a negative result. So trust that God has a better way. Make self-control an important part of your life.

> God knows that having self-control without him in our lives is next to impossible. But he wants us to master self-control, and he promises to help us get there.

Let's Talk about It . . .

What are some situations where you struggle to have self-control? Talk through some of the ways you can respond instead of reacting to the situation.

Let's Pray . . .

Dear God,
Thank you that self-control is a fruit of the Spirit
that you promise to help us with. When we are in a
situation where our emotions are triggered, please
help us to turn to you for guidance and self-control.
Amen.

Let's Act . . .

- Have a game night. If you have (or can purchase) the Jenga game, playing it can help teach self-control in many ways. Players have to remove the pieces in a controlled physical manner or the whole tower will come tumbling down. They also have to stay calm throughout the entire game. If they lose, they get to practice keeping control of their emotions, especially if they are very competitive (which is always a big test for our family!).

- For this activity, you only need yourselves and something to play music on. Have a "freeze" dance party. Designate someone to control the music, and while it's playing, just have fun and dance. When the music stops, everyone has to freeze in place. If you move, you're out. The last person standing wins. This game is a great exercise in making yourself take a breath and practice self-control.

- Last but not least, your family can play one of the favorite games in the Dooley household, which is Simon Says. One person (called "Simon") is designated as the direction specialist. Everyone else has to listen to the directions given by Simon. However, if Simon does not say, "Simon says," before giving the directions and you still do what they say, you are out. Have fun with Simon Says (and other games) and enjoy making memories with one another while also practicing self-control.

ACTIONS SPEAK LOUDER THAN WORDS

Do not merely listen to the word, and so deceive yourselves. Do what it says. Anyone who listens to the word but does not do what it says is like someone who looks at his face in a mirror and, after looking at himself, goes away and immediately forgets what he looks like. But whoever looks intently into the perfect law that gives freedom, and continues in it—not forgetting what they have heard, but doing it—they will be blessed in what they do.

James 1:22–25

Let's Think about It . . .

Have you ever been in church, Sunday school, or a Bible study and heard a message or lesson that seemed to be totally directed at you? How did you feel? And how did you respond? Did you allow it to change your life, or did you ignore it or forget about it and go on doing things the way you've been doing them all along? Have you ever met other Christians who say they read the Bible, go to church, memorize Scripture, and yet do not seem to follow the Scripture they recite? How does this make you feel? In our verse above, James is telling you that you must hear, think about, and then apply to your life what you read and learn about Jesus and his teachings in the Bible.

Let's Get into It . . .

As a young Christian in college, I struggled with acting on what the Bible was teaching me. I would read the Bible like a normal book at times and not apply it to my life. I called myself a Christian, but my actions could confuse those who saw me because of the inconsistent way I lived as a believer in Christ. Sometimes my temper would get the best of me and not represent Jesus or the wisdom of Ecclesiastes 7:9: "Do not be quickly provoked in your spirit, for anger resides in the lap of fools."

One particular moment in college truly impacted my life. As I was walking home from a Bible study, I passed a party at a nearby bar. I couldn't resist going in, but when I was inside, I looked around and immediately felt like I was not supposed to be there. I sat down by myself. I was holding my Bible and feeling so confused, and I asked myself, *Why are you here when you feel like you shouldn't be?* I knew in that moment that I had to change how I read the Bible and become more intentional about applying God's Word in my life.

Let's Learn . . .

When someone shows you how to do something—like make your bed or kick a soccer ball or bake cookies—you need to make sure you pay attention and follow their instructions so you will be able to do it well on your own. This is also how you should approach learning from the Bible. Pay attention and follow the instructions.

Reading the Bible shouldn't just be something to check off your to-do list. The Bible isn't like any other book. We aren't supposed to just read it to get information; we're supposed to read it and allow it to change us. It feels good when we finally make time to read our Bibles, but if we read them without making changes in our lives, we are not doing it right. As we learn more about Jesus, we should be inspired to live like him and be bright lights in a dark world. Reading God's Word helps us become like Jesus. It's like a cheat sheet for life. The Bible tells us exactly how we should live.

It's important to add worship, prayer, and listening to the Holy Spirit to your time of reading the Bible. All of these things help you apply God's Word to your everyday life. There is a blessing for those who can read God's Word, and their actions will be changed when they do what the Bible says. The Bible is a like a mirror held up to our lives. It shows us how we act toward other people, and it tells us if our actions are right or wrong. Without having God's Word to measure our actions against, we may not realize we are acting inappropriately toward others. The Bible's goal is to help us move past just reading about how we should live to living out those words with our actions.

Kids, it's one thing to read in the Bible that you are to honor your parents, but if you disrespect them, yell at them, talk back to them, or dishonor them in any way, you are not a doer of the word. Husbands, if you read in the Bible about how to honor your wife and treat her as an equal and yet you talk down to her, insult her with your words and actions, or dishonor her in any other way, then you are not a doer. And not being a doer hinders your prayers and may be blocking your blessings. And wives, the Bible says to love your husbands and children. Remember that God will help you do all these things, even when it feels hard.

God wants us to be more than hearers of the word; he also wants us to be doers. Our actions can speak louder than our words.

Let's Talk about It . . .

What are some of the things the Bible tells you to do? How can you be a person of action who does what the Bible tells you to do instead of just reading it?

Let's Pray . . .

Dear God,
Thank you for giving us your Word and your instructions on how to act. Help us to learn how to live and to bury the Scriptures deep within our hearts so we can become a Christian family of action. Amen.

- This fun activity brings to life what it means to be a doer and not just a hearer. It works best if a parent leads the activity and explains to the kids what the chocolate syrup, the stirring, and the milk represent.

1. Fill a clear glass three-fourths full of milk.
2. Next add some chocolate syrup, but don't stir it.
3. Explain that the chocolate syrup poured into the glass represents God's Word, Bible studies, church sermons, faith-based podcasts, Sunday school messages—anywhere you hear God's Word. The milk represents you. When the chocolate syrup is poured into the milk, it sits at the bottom of the glass and the milk in the glass still looks white.
4. Explain that the ingredients in the glass won't turn into chocolate milk until you stir the chocolate syrup and get it moving. The stirring represents how we should pray to the Holy Spirit for understanding as we apply God's Word to our lives. Then we should actually do something in response to what we are learning!
5. Enjoy the glass of chocolate milk!

- As a family, make a list of ways you can get into your community and live out your faith. You can help at a beach cleanup, do chores for a neighbor, share the produce from your garden with people who need fresh fruits and veggies, bake cookies for your stressed-out teacher, take care of another family's kids, or volunteer to help with the babies or toddlers at your church.

15

BETTER TOGETHER

Let us consider how we may spur one another on toward love and good deeds, not giving up meeting together, as some are in the habit of doing, but encouraging one another—and all the more as you see the Day approaching.

Hebrews 10:24–25

Let's Think about It . . .

Would you rather spend time with friends or family or by yourself? Do you enjoy learning about the Bible with others? How often do you spend time talking about Jesus with others? Do you challenge each other to follow God's directions and to become better Christians? Is it fun to learn about Jesus with others? Or do you sometimes forget and instead spend your time arguing with others, being negative, or pouting all alone?

After I graduated from college, I moved to San Diego, California. The first six months were pretty tough because I moved in with roommates I didn't know. I was blessed to have Christian roommates, but I was still finding my way—trying to find a job and make a living in a new state. Although I had people to share my house with, I still found myself feeling lonely and excluded because of the transition. I would read my Bible on my own, but I was missing community. I finally found a church where I felt connected to peers around my age who spent time together getting to know one another while learning more about Jesus. That was when I realized the importance of community and spending time with others. It's great to have your alone time, but don't do life alone.

Let's Learn . . .

It's always important to take inventory of our family dynamics. Are we spending enough quality time together as a family? Have we let video games, television, social media, tablets, work tasks, and computers increase division in our homes? We all need to pay attention to our daily lives and actions and consider how we interact with one another. The Bible is clear that people are important. We need each other. We need small groups where we become friends. We need to have fun and grow in our faith with other people. And this starts with the family.

Today's Scripture passage instructs us to "spur one another on toward love and good deeds." We can do this by finding ways to ignite a desire to love others as Christ loved us. God wants us to inspire other believers and to have an impact on our communities, including the less fortunate, the lost, the hurting, and those who need to hear the good news of Jesus Christ. We are better together when we can challenge each other to be more like Christ instead of challenging each other to anger, anxiety, and disagreement—all of which drive people away from each other and cause loneliness.

Family members should be friends with one another. And from there, each person in the family can attract other people to become friends with us. Together we should work to build healthy relationships that will last, both inside and outside the family. Doing devotions and reading the Bible together, along with participating in small groups and Bible studies, should be fun. When you take time to hang out and do life with one another as a family and with small groups of other people, we get to enjoy two things: engaging in activities that are fun and getting to know others better. In fact, the best way to make friends is by sharing experiences together. This is also a great way to live out the gospel message. We are all better together!

> God wants us to strengthen our spiritual lives by spending time with other believers and learning and growing together. It is better to live life in community with others than to be alone.

Let's Talk about It . . .

Now that you understand the importance of spending time with others, do you think it's better to live life with other people or alone? Talk about some of the ways life is better together.

Let's Pray . . .

Dear God,
Thank you that we don't have to live life on our own. When we have others around us helping us live a better life, it's so much easier to do the right things. Help us remember that life is better together. Amen.

Let's Act . . .

- List all the things you would like to do together as a family. Dream as big as you can because you never know what God can do! Write down all the places you would like to visit—a favorite restaurant, an amusement park, the beach, a stunning hiking spot, a museum, an athletic competition, another city or state or even country. Then find a place in the house where you can hang up the list. Put it where everyone will see it throughout the day. And plan how to make some of these dream outings a reality.

- Also make a list of small things you can do together as a family at home. You can write down things like planting a garden, having a movie night with popcorn and brownies, going on a family bike ride, roasting marshmallows in a backyard firepit, or packing a picnic for a day at the lake. Then take time to make memories together.

- If you don't yet belong to a local church, find a good one and get connected. It can take time to find the right church that fits your entire family. But once you have found it, find out about their small groups and join one so you can get connected with other believers who will help you grow in Christ. And make sure you get involved in the kids programs as well. It's fun to do things together as a family, but it's also fun to have your own friendships with believers who are in your same age group.

16

LOSS

> The LORD is close to the
> brokenhearted
> and saves those who are crushed in
> spirit.
>
> **Psalm 34:18**

Let's Think about It . . .

Have you had to deal with loss in your life? Have you lost a family member, a friend, or someone else who was important to you? Has a situation in your community, your country, or around the world made you sad? The grief and pain of loss look different for everyone. We all react to loss in our own way. But we all have the same source of comfort available to us—God.

Let's Get into It . . .

The hurt you feel when you lose someone you love is real. The loss isn't easy to get over. It's hard to be your complete self when you lose a piece of yourself in the form of a friend or family member. I lost my father to

COVID-19 in August 2020. The process leading up to his passing was agonizing. My dad suffered from a lot of health issues, and I hated watching him suffer.

However, nothing could compare to the traumatizing couple of months when he was battling this virus. He spent almost a month on a ventilator, and his condition never improved. During that time, it was easy to think, *God, where are you?*—especially when my dad would tell me, "I can't wait to have a new body." I had mixed feelings when he said that because I was often praying and believing for a miracle in his earthly body. Eventually, the doctors' last efforts to save him through a tracheotomy failed.

My dad was one of my best friends. He was my very first superhero. My father was the purest example of a great man, husband, pastor, and lover of people I had in my life. Through his actions, he modeled the importance of family and showed us how special a family could be. In his last days, I was very sad, but I still felt God's presence. I didn't want to lose my dad, and yet I felt a peace come over me—feelings that could only come from a loving spiritual Father.

Let's Learn . . .

Death never feels good when you lose someone close to you. In history, there was only one death that hurt at first but then brought on rejoicing three days later. Jesus was sent to earth with a mission—to give us an opportunity to live in heaven for eternity. His death conquered Satan and sin's rule over us and brought salvation for those of us who truly believe in Jesus as our Savior.

Dealing with grief without the help of the Lord is so hard for me to comprehend. Memories of the loved ones you have lost can be triggered in so many ways and can immediately bring you back to the moment when they were here and spending time with you. These moments are really hard, but God is here to help us. He wants us to give our pain, worry, concern, and care to him. The Bible promises us that the Lord is near. Sometimes when we encounter tough times, we feel like God is nowhere to be found. But he always knows when you are hurting, and he is right there to wrap his loving arms around you and comfort you.

If you can trust, and have faith in the Lord, you will have God's heart-healing strength during your broken times and experience the miracle of having God in your life. In my father's passing, a miracle did take place. He had to be revived twice on Friday, and by Saturday he had stabilized. On Sunday morning, my mother sent me a text message asking if we could do a Google Duo chat with Dad because he wanted to speak to my brother and me. I had the opportunity to see him and talk to him fifteen minutes before he would leave this earth. I know he has a new body and that one day in heaven I will see him again, but this loss is still hard. However, I know that God always gives hope and love, even in the hardest moments of life.

> God is our comforter in times of loss. He comes alongside us and gives us his love and his presence. When our hearts are broken, we can always count on God to pick us up and put us back together again.

Let's Talk about It . . .

Can you think of a time when you lost somebody who was close to you or when you were hurt and sad? How did you feel? How did God help you through your grief and pain?

Let's Pray . . .

Dear God,
Thank you for being near us and always giving us
comfort in life's hardest moments. Help us turn to
you when we experience loss of any kind in our lives.
Amen.

Let's Act . . .

- It can be very hard to talk about loss, but it's an important step to take in the healing process. If your family is dealing with loss or a very sad situation, talk together about what's happening. Give every person a chance to share what they are feeling and what has been the hardest part for them. Then pray for one another and ask God to help you during this time of grief, pain, and heartbreak.
- Find some verses in the Bible that talk about how God gives us comfort in hard times. Read these verses together when your family is experiencing a difficult situation. Hug each other and let God comfort you as you comfort one another.

17

HAVING INTEGRITY

> The righteous lead blameless lives;
> blessed are their children after
> them.
>
> **Proverbs 20:7**

Let's Think about It . . .

Do you ever lie to other people? Do you sometimes keep the truth from your friends or family members or someone else you spend time with? When you are by yourself and nobody is watching, do you act the same way you do in public? Nobody is perfect, and nobody always does the right thing. If you make mistakes, you are not a bad person. You're actually in a great place to learn to live a life of *integrity*.

Let's Get into It . . .

My father would continually tell my brother and me to be men of integrity, to be the same person we are behind closed doors as we are in public. That advice rang loud in my head when I was leaving a grocery store. I realized when I got to the car that I was given more money than I should have received back in change. Initially, I thought, *It was their mistake, and I'm in a hurry.* However, I was reminded that I want to be a man of integrity who should do the right thing and go back into the store and let the cashier know. So I went back in and stood in line so I could let her know she gave me more money by accident. Once I told her what happened, she could not believe I came back. She poured out her thanks because that error would have gotten her into trouble.

Let's Learn . . .

A person who has integrity is a person who is honest and has a strong desire to always do what is right. Almost everyone respects people who have integrity, including people who aren't Christians. Integrity is attractive, disarming, and beautiful. Integrity builds trust. And integrity starts from the inside. Matthew 12:34 says, "You brood of vipers, how can you who are evil say anything good? For the mouth speaks what the heart is full of." In other words, what you say behind closed doors about people, beliefs and actions, world issues, or anything else matters. Your words show what is in your heart. Words are a window to what is inside a person, which can range from good to bad. Everything starts with your heart, including having integrity.

Did you know you can never fool God? He already knows what is in your heart. What God wants most of all is to help us clean up our hearts. And we can start by paying attention to our words. Our words can be used to hurt others or to help others. When we intentionally plant our hearts with the good seeds that come from following Jesus, we will reap a harvest of good things—including good words. The sooner we realize that we are imperfect, flawed human beings who need a Savior, the sooner true change can take place in our lives. And with that will come words and actions that show the good things in our hearts.

Today's Scripture reminds us that the children of those who do right will be happy. Kids reap the benefits of their parents' right living. Words and actions and decisions that are in line with what God wants will always have a positive influence on others. Also, remember that you are never too young to apply God's Word to your own life and influence others around you to be more like Christ. When you talk the talk and match it by walking the walk, you show you have integrity.

Living a life of integrity takes humility and courage. However, you do not have to come up with the strength to do this alone. Lean on Jesus when you feel weak. Ask him to give you the strength to pursue a life of integrity. Parents, remember that your actions of integrity directly influence your children's futures. Set a godly standard now, and you will leave a lasting legacy you can be proud of.

> God wants us to live a life of integrity. He wants us to do the right thing, no matter who we are with or who is watching us.

Let's Talk about It . . .

Now that you have learned a little more about the word *integrity*, can you explain in your own words what it means to have integrity? Can you share an example from your own life where you acted with integrity?

Dear God,
Please help our actions to match our words. When
this happens, we show we have integrity and can
more easily point others toward you. Amen.

Let's Act . . .

- It's not easy to live a life of integrity without the Lord. You want to be a family that talks the talk and walks the walk of goodness, humility, and integrity. Pray together daily that God will teach your family to be pure of heart and to live a life that is pleasing to him. You can make this a regular part of your family prayer time.

- Playing games together is a great way to practice acting with integrity. Sometimes you may feel tempted to cheat or to get mad during a game, but work hard to not let that happen. Whether you're playing basketball or card games or tag, play by the rules, try your best, encourage others, and be a good sport. Play with integrity.

- Talk about people you know who have integrity. They may be people you know, or they may be famous people who live for Jesus. How do they show they have integrity? Where does their strength come from? What can you do to be more like them?

18

BAD COMPANY

Do not be misled: "Bad company corrupts good character."

1 Corinthians 15:33

? Let's Think about It . . .

Think about the people you see every day—at school, at work, in the neighborhood, in other places you go. Can you tell who are the nice people and who are the mean ones? Have you ever had people in your life whom you kept around as friends, even though you knew deep down they were a bad influence on you? Have you ever experienced a time when you thought someone was your friend but turned out not to be? It isn't always easy to know when someone is truly a nice person and when they are just pretending to be nice. That's why we need God's wisdom in making good choices about the people we spend time with.

Let's Get into It . . .

I have four kids, and all of them have different personalities. One of my kids is a social butterfly. She has a beautiful heart and spirit, and she likes to include everyone, meet everyone, and be loved by everyone. It's adorable to watch and also alarming. Parents never want to see their children get hurt, and when someone like my daughter is so open and friendly and loving, they can easily get hurt.

Let's Learn . . .

I want to be clear about something. We should show love to everyone, but we get to choose who we spend time with. And not everyone you meet is right for you. We need to remember that all of us can be influenced in some way by other people—neighbors, people at the gym, kids you go to school with, coworkers, people on your sports teams, kids who do the same activities you do, people in your church, influencers you follow online, actors in the TV shows and movies you watch, characters in the books you read. That's why it's important to remember the warning in today's Bible verse. If you are spending a lot of time with people who don't follow Jesus and aren't aligned with your beliefs, it will eventually affect the way you act.

If you call yourself a Christian, you have a different set of standards to live by. We all live in this world, but as Christians we are not to be *of* this world. Now this doesn't mean we can get upset with or judge non-Christians. Their belief system is different from ours. We are to be a light in this world. Our job is to show the light of God to people who aren't believers. So if you spend a lot of time with people who aren't Christians, remember that their moral compass will be different from yours. They may say and do things that don't align with God. And if you are at a weak point in your life and aren't as connected to God as you should be, you could allow yourself to be pulled into doing and saying what they are doing and saying.

Other people can sway your decision making. And one wrong decision can change your life. I knew a devout Christian guy who was kind and funny. He had great parents who were pastors, and he was an amazing athlete. But when he got to college, he struggled with wanting to hang out with guys who lived a completely different lifestyle. As he hung out with them, he started to become more and more influenced by them and found himself feeling angry and depressed. His new "friends" were making fun of him, which was having an awful effect on his life.

He then decided to buy a gun so he could take revenge on one of his teammates who had pushed him to the limits of embarrassment and anger. But something nudged him to stop by another friend's dorm room before he moved ahead with a horrible crime. The friend reminded him of who he truly was—a child of God, a young man called to serve the God he loved. This act ultimately stopped him from committing a sin that would have ruined his life.

I am so very thankful my friend talked me out of doing something so deeply irresponsible, something that could have had a tragic ending. My life would look so different right now if I hadn't had good Christian friends like him in my life.

It's a beautiful thing to love all people, but not all people love or respect who you represent. Not everyone is going to like you, but nobody will ever love you as much as God does. Be careful with the company you keep, and always make sure God is your number one.

God wants us to be careful about who we spend time with. The best kind of company is other believers who are also walking with Jesus.

Who are the main people you spend time with right now? Are these people followers of Christ? Are they an influence for good? Do you think God might want you to change who you are close friends with?

Let's Pray . . .

Dear God,
Thank you for bringing friends and other people into our lives. Please help us to make good decisions about the people we choose to get close to. Amen.

Let's Act . . .

- Have a family conversation about friendship. Ask everyone who their friends are and who they are choosing to spend their time with. Then answer these questions to decide if these are friendships worth investing in: Why do you call this person your friend? Are they consistently nice to you and to others? Do they make you feel happy or sad? Do they make you feel good about yourself, or do they often hurt your feelings? Pray that everyone in the family will make good friendships, especially friendships with other Christians.
- While it's fun to have one best friend, it's also fun to have family friendships. Find a few families in church you have things in common with. Maybe you like the same types of

activities. Maybe the kids are all super close in age. Maybe the family just seems nice and fun. Invite them to hang out. Go out to lunch together after church. Visit a park together. Have them over to dinner. Great friendships begin with someone reaching out.

19

FAMILY CARE

> Because so many people were coming and going that they did not even have a chance to eat, he said to them, "Come with me by yourselves to a quiet place and get some rest."
>
> **Mark 6:31**

Let's Think about It . . .

Do you feel tired sometimes? Do you ever feel like you need a break from your friends or family members? Does school or work or other activities or responsibilities sometimes drain you? Do you ever feel like there is not enough time in a day to do all the things you want (or need) to do? Do you ever feel like you are underwater, fighting to stay afloat between juggling work or school, friends, activities, hobbies, chores, exercising, and just living life? In all of the craziness of life, how are you taking care of yourself? *Are* you taking care of yourself?

Let's Get into It . . .

Our family has a busy household. It seems like it is never quiet in our home until everyone is asleep. With four kids (and two active parents) running around the house, things can feel chaotic. Sometimes when I walk into our house, I feel like I'm arriving at the Seahawks stadium during a game and mouthing to my wife from a distance, "Hey, babe!" Like I said, we are a busy family!

Let's Learn . . .

If we do not find a way to unwind, get away, have alone time, recharge, and rest, we will not really be much good to others. We will not have the bandwidth to endure the cares of each day. An unrested family member (I'm looking at you, Mom or Dad) will create an unhealthy family dynamic. Even Jesus needed to get away from everyone to rest and pray in isolation. Jesus was pulled left and right as he preached, taught, led, and healed. He attracted crowds everywhere he went. He was dealing with people and their issues all the time.

If Jesus needed time away, so do we. We have to remember we are mere human beings. The Bible reminds us that we need rest because we are not God, and when we are feeling weak, we need his supernatural strength. Jesus understands what our human bodies go through because he is fully God and also fully human.

My wife and I realized that since we have been married, neither of us has taken time away from everyone else in the family (including each other) for our own individual rest and recharge.

This was a powerful revelation we had to do something about. My wife was trying her hardest to keep it together, but she was home with the kids 24-7. She was missing her alone time, feeling overwhelmed, and trying to figure out who she had been before she became a mom. I was missing my own alone time as I was feeling the weight of the world on my shoulders to provide for and take care of my family and to lead them the way God wants me to. My wife and I lost our fathers within ten months of each other, and I went right back to work without taking a breather. This isn't the way God wants us to live.

This was not the best example for us to set for our kids. Plus, kids need parents who are healthy, engaged, and loving. If you're a kid with brothers and sisters, you need your own individual space too. No matter how old you are, you need to take care of yourself. It's okay to spend time alone. Remember, even Jesus needed to take a break from his ministry and from loving others to spend time with the Father.

> God wants to take care of us and to help us avoid feeling overwhelmed, and one way to do this is to take care of ourselves.

Let's Talk about It . . .

What situations make you feel overwhelmed and in need of getting away? Do you take a break when this happens? What kind of break makes you feel rested and ready to jump back into things again?

Let's Pray . . .

Dear God,
Thank you for showing us how Jesus took time for
himself to rest and pray. Help us to do the same
thing when the demands of life get to be too over-
whelming. Amen.

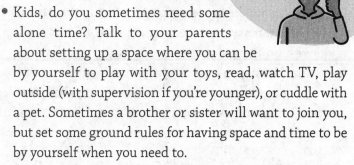

Let's Act . . .

- Kids, do you sometimes need some alone time? Talk to your parents about setting up a space where you can be by yourself to play with your toys, read, watch TV, play outside (with supervision if you're younger), or cuddle with a pet. Sometimes a brother or sister will want to join you, but set some ground rules for having space and time to be by yourself when you need to.

- Put together a family recharge plan. My wife and I have planned a quarterly hotel getaway. It's nothing elaborate, but we will take turns spending twenty-four hours alone by ourselves in a hotel room. This is our own individual time to get away from everything—to pray, relax, read, walk around town, visit a coffee shop, work out, play video games, draw, sleep, or just do nothing. Maybe for you it's an afternoon or an evening alone, when you can get a babysitter and take time to think, breathe, and listen to God. For our kids, we try to allow them moments to get away from everyone else in the house so they can have some alone time. While we may not do this a lot, we do try to discern when they need to have some healthy time by themselves.

⇒20⇐

APPRECIATE YOUR FAMILY

Children, obey your parents in
everything, for this pleases the Lord.

Colossians 3:20

Let's Think about It . . .

Kids, is it hard for you to listen to your parents at
times? When you are asked to stop doing something, do you listen and obey right away? Do you
want to have a good life? Parents, do you ever feel
so overwhelmed that you lose sight of the blessings you do have?
Do you ever feel like life's negatives outweigh the positives?
Do you sometimes forget what a blessing it is to have a family? Do you also want to have a good life?

Let's Get into It . . .

I've watched my kids ask my wife if they could
have some chips—right after I told them, "No, you
can't have chips right now." Thank goodness my wife and I have
finally learned to ask the kids, "Did you already ask your dad?"

93

or "Did you already ask your mom?" Then we ask them what the other parent said. We had to drive home the fact that Mom and Dad are *one*. This is important because when we discipline and teach our kids, we want to give them a clear message. When there is division, there is confusion. But when there is unity, there is clarity and strength.

Let's Learn . . .

Not every family looks the same. We don't all look alike. We come from different places. Some families are big, and some families are small. Not all families have grandparents and cousins, and some families all live under one roof. However, no matter what it looks like, a Christian household can be a beautiful thing when it is running the way God intended it to. And that starts with obedience. The Bible is very clear on obedience. Obeying pleases the Lord. Now, kids will not just naturally know how to obey. They have to be taught this. (Parents have to keep practicing obedience too!)

In the book of Colossians, the Bible teaches us how to run a home and family. The key is to make Jesus the center of our home. A true home is not just a roof over our heads and a place to stay. It's a place where Jesus lives. That is why it is important that we read our Bibles individually and aloud together as a family. That's how we learn how to listen to the Holy Spirit, how to pray, and how to live like Christ. It is vital for a family to be on the same page with God and with each other. And Mom and Dad need to be on the same team here. Otherwise, the kids may try to trick or control the parents in unhealthy ways. (Remember the chips story?)

Kids, trust Mom and Dad when they tell you to follow certain instructions. They love you and have your best interests at heart. When your parents tell you to stop running ahead of them, to watch out for cars, or to stop fighting with brothers or sisters or friends, listen to them and obey. Your parents want you to be safe and secure. They are looking out for you. It is your parents' duty to raise you the way God wants you raised.

Jesus set an example for us when he obeyed his earthly parents. And the Ten Commandments tell us to honor our mother and our father so that we may live a long life (see Exodus 20:12). So don't scream at your parents. Don't talk bad about your parents. Don't disobey your parents on purpose. The only time you can disobey your parents is if they tell you to disobey God.

Parents, I encourage you to read Colossians 3:21, which talks about not making your kids bitter, because although they are instructed to obey, we are to correct them with love. We are not to make them feel resentful or angry and hostile toward us. We are to teach them how to willingly want to obey because it's the godly thing to do. When your kids are motivated to honor you and please the Lord, they will bring blessings and joy to your home.

> God wants kids to obey and honor their parents.
> He also wants parents to recognize that their
> kids are a blessing and treat them that way.

Let's Talk about It . . .

How is the obedience situation in your home these days? Kids, do you obey your parents? Parents, are you asking for God's guidance on how to raise your kids, and are you showing them God's love?

Let's Pray . . .

Dear God,
Since the Bible tells us that Jesus is to be the center
of our home, please help us all to remember this and
to obey you and your commands. Amen.

Let's Act . . .

- If obedience has been an issue in your home, have a family conversation about the importance of obedience. Maybe the kids feel like the rules aren't super clear. Maybe the parents feel like the kids choose to consistently disobey. Talk honestly about what you expect from one another, and come up with a game plan for making it easier to obey. Then pray that God will help everyone start to change.

- Go on a family bike ride together. Before you set out on your bikes, talk about how, while biking, you should obey certain rules and guidelines to help keep you safe. For example, make sure everyone in the family wears a helmet. Check to see that the brakes on everyone's bike are working. When you're on the road, follow the rules. Bike single file when you need to. Stop at stop signs and traffic lights. Ride on the correct side of the road. If you get too far ahead of the group, stop and wait for everyone else. Following the rules keeps you safe while still allowing you to have fun!

21

SIN ON PURPOSE

If we deliberately keep on sinning after we have received the knowledge of the truth, no sacrifice for sins is left, but only a fearful expectation of judgment and of raging fire that will consume the enemies of God.

Hebrews 10:26–27

? Let's Think about It . . .

Have you ever been told by someone not to do something and you did it anyway, despite knowing that the other person would not like it? Do you think you are stubborn? Do you tend to deliberately do things you know you shouldn't do? If you answered yes to any of these questions, you have committed a sinful act willingly, which is not what God wants us to do.

Let's Get into It . . .

When I was around six years old, I remember going into a store in Columbus, Ohio, called Super

Duper. I wanted a pack of gum; however, my parents had already told me no. But I wanted that pack of gum so bad. In fact, nothing anyone could have said to me at that moment would have kept me from getting it. Either my parents were going to change their minds and surprise me with it, or I was going to get the five-finger discount and walk away with the pack of gum in my back pocket.

I asked my mom again for the gum, and she said, "No." Mom kept walking, and I did the unspeakable. I grabbed the gum and slipped it into my back pocket. I thought I was going to walk out of the Super Duper without any consequences. But when we got to the checkout line, the cashier looked at me and said, "Hey, little guy. Are you going to pay for that?" My mom looked down at me and said, "That better not be that pack of gum." My ears felt warm, and I had sweat on my nose. I knew I was in trouble. Long story short, I had to give the gum back and feel really embarrassed, and then I had to deal with the discipline from my parents. Not fun.

Let's Learn . . .

When Christians commit sin on purpose, it is heartbreaking to the Lord. The reason it's a big deal is because sin comes from a stubborn and rebellious place. When you sin, you are essentially saying you don't care what the Lord thinks and that you are going to commit this sin anyway.

The Bible tells us we face consequences for our deliberate sinful actions. God will always help correct a defiant spirit. The writer of Hebrews says, "God disciplines us for our good, in order that we may share in his holiness" (12:10). As Christians, we should know better than to sin on purpose. Just because we can't lose our salvation over it doesn't mean we can live recklessly, deciding we can just repent whenever we want to. That is a terrible way to live.

As a follower of Christ, you have an advantage in this life. You have the power of God working inside you to help you overcome temptations that would have devoured you in the past. You have a supernatural Father you can call on who will help you prevail in the present.

It will always be Satan's mission to test, tempt, and trip you up. But you don't have to give in. You don't have to copy what other people are doing. If you know that what they are doing is wrong, choose to be like Jesus. Choose to be strong. Choose to set a good example. Choose to make a positive impact on others.

It should be our mission to focus on Jesus, take snapshots of his Word, download them into our spirit, and witness the change from sinning on purpose to purposely not wanting to sin at all.

**God does not want us to sin on purpose.
That's why it is important to stay connected
to him and practice obeying his word.**

Let's Talk about It . . .

Can you think of a time when you were really tempted to sin, even though you knew it was 100 percent the wrong thing to do? How did you handle the situation? And how can you make sure you do the right thing next time?

Let's Pray . . .

Dear God,
The Bible makes it clear that we are to do our best
not to sin. Sometimes it can be really hard to do the
right thing, but please give us strength when we are
tempted to do wrong. Amen.

Let's Act . . .

- Make it a family habit to say nightly prayers together. Bedtime is perfect for taking a little extra time to talk to God and reflect on how the day went. It's also a good time to remember the things you did wrong, confess them to God, ask for his forgiveness, and ask for his help so you can do the right thing tomorrow. You can also talk together about ongoing temptations and struggles and pray about those things.

- The Bible tells us we are stronger together. That's why having a prayer partner and someone to talk honestly with can be a really good thing. Mom and Dad, it's natural for you to be each other's partners. Or choose a close friend or relative. Kids can choose a brother or sister or a best friend or a parent. With your partner, have meaningful conversations about your walk with Christ. Maybe you and your partner go out to breakfast or lunch once a month, or you set a special time to hang out together at home. You can even text each other throughout the day to check in and see how the other person is doing.

22

WE NEED YOU

> Heal me, LORD, and I will be healed;
> save me and I will be saved,
> for you are the one I praise.
>
> **Jeremiah 17:14**

? Let's Think about It . . .

We're going to talk about a difficult topic—the problems that come when someone is addicted, when they feel like they need something (a drug, alcohol, or other things) in order to survive. It can affect someone physically or emotionally, and it can be painful to break that dependence. Has anyone in your family or any friends of your family struggled with addiction or drug abuse? Have they overcome their addiction, or are they still struggling with it? How do you feel as you see that person in pain and in a bad place in their life?

Let's Get into It . . .

Addiction comes in many forms and can be draining. As a youth pastor, I spent time with a lot of young people and enjoyed being able to be in their lives. But I was also reminded regularly about the struggles so many of them deal with. One of the high schoolers in our group told me his brother had an addiction that started after a knee injury on the football field. His brother was given pain medicine by a friend of his, and he became addicted to it, causing him a long battle with drugs. We prayed for him and tried to get him help. Tragically, he ultimately lost his battle with addiction and died.

Let's Learn . . .

It can be tough to watch people we love suffer and to feel like we can't help them. Addiction is hard on the person who is suffering from it, as well as on the people around them. Addiction can ruin friendships and entire families. I hope you are not dealing with this issue at home. But even if you are not, you may know a family who is dealing with it. It is important to have compassion for the individuals who are fighting this difficult battle.

If someone close to your family is battling addiction, there is hope. God gives everyone the chance for redemption and restoration. No problem is too big for our God. Everyone falls short at times, and we all need strength from our heavenly Father to overcome our problems. In today's Bible verse, Jeremiah knows that God is the only one who can give him true healing and save him. We may have physical diseases and illnesses we would like God to heal, which he can do. However, the most important thing is to get to the root of the sin we continually commit.

If you don't know Jesus on a personal level and haven't asked him to be the center of your life, you can pray for spiritual healing and ask God to forgive your sin. Once you have given your life to Christ, you have taken the most important step toward true healing.

Parents, if one or both of you is the one suffering from addiction or drug abuse, this next section is for you. You will need to follow the practical steps from medical professionals who will be able to help you with recovery. Your children need you. God has blessed you with little human beings who have a part to play in the big picture of God's plan. Parents have a huge responsibility to steward and shape these future world changers. We can't be selfish and neglect our parenting duties. Our children deserve the best. And our best comes from the leading of the Lord and being in a healthy relationship with him.

Misusing drugs or alcohol can be tormenting, destructive, and deadly. Nobody can fight it alone, and we need people, help, and Jesus to overcome it. If the words you read here apply to you or your spouse, please get help. If you are not dealing with these issues but know someone who needs help, point that person in the right direction for restoration.

Finally, if this situation does not apply to you or anyone close to you, take a moment to pray for those who are struggling with these very real issues. Many people are dealing with addiction, and they need your prayers. Imagine a world that prays for others and doesn't just think about themselves. Imagine a world that wants to see families win. Imagine a world where addiction starts to decrease as a result of the power of prayer. You have the power to align with God and plead with him on behalf of people around the world.

> God does not want any of us to suffer from addiction. While people can make big mistakes, God can provide life-changing help and healing.

Let's Talk about It . . .

How close to home does this topic hit? This is a highly sensitive subject, and it may be one for just the adults (or maybe the adults and older kids in the family) to talk about. No matter how you choose to handle it, make God and prayer the focus of how you deal with it.

Let's Pray . . .

Dear God,
A lot of people in this world struggle with addiction and substance abuse. Please help these people overcome their struggles. Surround them with experienced professionals who can get them back to living a clean life. Also, please help our family to support them. Amen.

Let's Act . . .

- Take this time to pray for your family, another family, or an unknown family who is dealing with substance abuse.
Familiarize yourself with resources so you can either get help for yourself or point others in the right direction. Does your church have resources for helping those who struggle with addiction? You can support those resources by giving money or volunteering your time. And keep praying. God can help anyone overcome anything!

23

QUITTING ISN'T AN OPTION

> The LORD makes firm the steps
> of the one who delights in him;
> though he may stumble, he will not fall,
> for the LORD upholds him with
> his hand.
>
> **Psalm 37:23–24**

Let's Think about It . . .

How many times have you heard someone say, "Do not quit"? How many times have you quit something? How many times have you pushed through the desire to quit and stuck with something? How did it feel when you felt like quitting and instead pushed through?

Let's Get into It . . .

I'm thankful that my parents taught me at a very young age not to quit. To be clear, they knew the limits and did not force me to do something or to participate in an event or sport if I did not have the desire to do it. However, if I *was* interested in a class, sport, event, or program, quitting was not an option. In our family, finishing what you started was the only option.

I wanted to throw in the towel on so many things—football, basketball, track, boxing, homework, trying to find something I had lost, friendships, school, church, jobs. It's normal to have those feelings. Everything can feel hard at times. But it's how you respond to the hard things that makes a lasting impression and affects your future.

Let's Learn . . .

How do you respond when you are overwhelmed? Do you want to just drop everything and quit? Do you slowly feel yourself drifting away and losing the motivation to carry on? If so, it's okay to have those thoughts. However, we shouldn't act on them. When we feel like quitting, we need to be reminded why we are doing what we are doing and to remember that we don't have to shoulder the burden all by ourselves.

Our two-year-daughter Ava looks as if she owns the street she is walking on. However, there are moments when she holds my hand as we head to our destination and her foot catches on a curb or rock and she trips. When she starts to fall, I tighten my grip on her hand to make sure she doesn't fall too hard and help her back up on her feet. This is what God does for us. We will go through hard times and will fall. We may not know how to get back up on our own, but God has his redeeming hand outstretched for us to grab so we can stand back up and continue on.

Kids, it may be hard to stick with something you have started. But take a moment and ask God for help. Believe that he will help you and that he has provided you with other people to help you. It may not be easy, but we have to look at God's bigger plan.

Being a Christian doesn't mean we will avoid suffering or discomfort. However, our pain is temporary. In the end, we win. We have an eternal destination we are headed toward. If we believe our strength comes from Christ, we know there is more to life than what happens here on earth.

When we feel like quitting, God wants us to get back up, keep going, and trust that he has our backs because we have a purpose to fulfill. If we quit, it can rob others of their blessings, and we are to be a blessing to others. And it can rob you of what God wants to be building into you. He is building character traits such as patience, faithfulness, self-control, and perseverance. Set an example to others and let them see how God can be trusted to help us through challenging times, as you choose not to quit when things get hard.

> God tells us he blesses those who do right. When
> you are frustrated and want to quit, know that
> God is on your side and will help you.

Let's Talk about It . . .

What are some things you want to quit right now? Do you think God wants you to keep doing these things? If the answer is yes, what can you do to have a more positive attitude and push through, and who can you talk with to get the help you might need?

Let's Pray . . .

Dear God,
We all need your help and your strength. Please help
us know what to do when we feel like quitting, and
please make our steps firm. Amen.

Let's Act . . .

- As a family, create a list of things you will not quit on. Write down these things, have everyone sign their name, and put up the list where everyone will see it. Help one another when things get hard and remind everyone, "This family does not quit!"
- What is something your family has always wanted to try but has been reluctant to do? Sometimes the best way to motivate yourself not to quit is to challenge yourself. You might sign up for a 5K run, learn to cook a new type of food, adopt a pet, choose a book series to read together, or start taking weekend hikes. Encourage each other to stick with the activity. You'll learn and grow together as you practice not quitting.

⇥24⇤

POWER OF YOUR WORDS

The tongue has the power of life
and death,
and those who love it will eat its fruit.

Proverbs 18:21

Let's Think about It . . .

Do you take time to really think about the words you say? Are there times when you say things you don't mean about yourself, your family, or your friends? Have you ever been in an argument and said something you wished you could take back? What about when mean words are directed at you? Do they hurt your feelings? And what about good words? How do you feel when someone says something nice to you or when you say something nice to someone else?

Let's Get into It . . .

Before I got married, I was given so much advice. Some of the advice was really good, and some of it I'm still trying to figure out. However, there was one piece of advice that has been a blessing to me, my wife, and my kids: make sure you wash your wife with words. In other words, shower her with positive words—speaking well of her, telling her how beautiful and talented and smart she is, reminding her what a great wife she is and what an amazing mom she is.

Let's Learn . . .

Our words have power. You can speak words to people and they may not believe them right away, but over time, if they hear the words enough, it can impact how they see themselves and change who they are. For instance, my wife is gorgeous. She is talented and gifted in teaching the Bible, and she is also a great wife and mother. She's always been beautiful and talented, but she would tell you she feels more beautiful now than she did in the past because of how I've washed her with my words. I don't do it in an insincere manner. I just make sure I am telling her consistently how wonderful she is.

Parents, if you tell your kids they are strong, obedient, intelligent, and all-around good kids, you will help shape who they are. And if you say three simple words, it will have a profound impact on their self-confidence, stability, and courage, and it will give them the ability to show love to others in the future. These three words are, "I love you."

Some kids go through life never once hearing their parents say "I love you." I never knew that was true until one day I was meeting with a high school guy in my youth group. As he was leaving, I told him, "I'm proud of you. I love you, bro." It stopped him in his tracks, and he turned around and teared up, saying, "No one has ever said they love me." I gave him his fist bump and said, "It's all love here, bro." We parted, and I was stunned by his words. I didn't realize that was a real thing. We can change that narrative.

The tongue holds the power of life and death. And just as speaking well about another person encourages them, the opposite is also true. Speaking badly about your parents, spouse, friends, kids, brothers and sisters, friends, coworkers, or even yourself can be very damaging. If you gossip, lie, speak unkindly about someone, call others bad names, or use your words as weapons, you are actually speaking death over others or yourself. That's why it's so important to think before you speak. If you don't, you may end up saying the wrong thing at the wrong time to the wrong person, who will be hurt because of your wrong words.

Words hold weight, which is why we need to watch what we say. Our words should revitalize others and build them up. We all know how it feels when people say mean things about us. Don't be the person who hurts other people's feelings. You have a choice to either build others up or tear them down with your words. In order to make the right choice, we need the power of the Holy Spirit.

God wants us to be careful with our words and to carefully think about what we are saying and how it will affect someone else before we open our mouths to speak.

Let's Talk about It . . .

Do you like to speak well of others, or do you find yourself talking negatively about other people? How do our words reflect what is in our hearts? How can we do better at being a family that speaks well of one another and of others.

Let's Pray . . .

Dear God,
Our words have so much power! Help us use them
to build others up rather than tear others down.
Please help us to speak well of others and to be a
family that encourages others and speaks words of
positivity. Amen.

Let's Act . . .

- Make a list of declarations that your family will speak over each other daily. Some ideas: *You are smart. You are kind. You are talented. You are beautiful. You are honest. You are a good friend. You are a hard worker.* Before bed or at breakfast or any time you are all together, speak these words over one another. You can even take it outside your family and start speaking these declarations to kids at school, coworkers, neighbors, friends, and anyone else you spend time with.

- As a family, memorize this verse that gives encouragement to recognize the power of words:

> Do not let any unwholesome talk come out of your mouths, but only what is helpful for building others up according to their needs, that it may benefit those who listen.
>
> **Ephesians 4:29**

25

GOD'S LOVE IS ETERNAL

Who shall separate us from the love of Christ? Shall trouble or hardship or persecution or famine or nakedness or danger or sword? . . . No, in all these things we are more than conquerors through him who loved us. For I am convinced that neither death nor life, neither angels nor demons, neither the present nor the future, nor any powers, neither height nor depth, nor anything else in all creation, will be able to separate us from the love of God that is in Christ Jesus our Lord.

Romans 8:35, 37–39

Let's Think about It . . .

Do you believe that God loves you? Do you think that God still loves you even if you are unkind to someone or do something wrong? Have you ever felt like God doesn't hear you? Does God sometimes feel far away? Do you wonder if your past actions have caused God not to love you anymore?

Let's Get into It . . .

My wife and I were at a parent-teacher confer-ence for our son, Andy II, when the teacher told us the most beautiful thing that had happened in class. A little girl in Andy's class had asked him, "Do you love me?" At five years old, our son eloquently said, "Yes, I do, and God loves you too." I want you to know, too, that no matter what you have done in the past, what you are doing in the present, or what you will do in the future, God loves you.

Let's Learn . . .

We all have our own issues and messes to deal with in our individual lives. I know that in my past, the things I did and said were not always pleasing to God. Even today, if I have not eaten enough or gotten enough sleep, I need Jesus more than ever so I don't say or do something I will regret. It is a constant battle for all of us. And Satan wants us to believe that if we mess up, God will fall out of love with us.

I've also been guilty of thinking that if a person commits a horrible crime, God will fall out of love with them. It is tough for me to watch or read the news and not be disturbed by the terrible things going on in our world today. However, I need to remember I'm not the judge. I only have control over myself. God is in control of everything, and his love is unconditional. We are imperfect human beings who live in an imperfect world, but we are loved by a perfect God whose love is perfect.

I love how today's Scripture passage lists so many different issues and possible ways for us to be separated from Christ, just so the main question can be answered: Who can separate us from the love of Christ? *No one!*

The Bible makes it clear that your past, your present, and your future cannot separate you from the love of our heavenly Father. The apostle Paul, the writer of this passage, mentions a few specific things he experienced. When Paul lived, if you confessed you were a Christian, you were made fun of, bullied, harassed, tormented, and mistreated. You could even be killed. Paul, who used to be named Saul before he met Jesus, had been a hater of Christians. It was not until he had a real encounter with God that his life was changed and he started living for the Lord. True change comes from the love of Christ. When we realize that God committed the ultimate sacrifice by allowing Jesus to die on the cross for our sins and that he gave us the chance to live for eternity, we will catch a glimpse of how much he loves us.

Now, knowing that Christ still loves you, no matter what you do, doesn't give you a license to sin on purpose. But it should excite you that Jesus is on your side. You are loved by someone who won't stop loving you, no matter what. Nobody in your life will ever love you the way God does.

There is nothing like the love of God. And if we put our faith in him, nothing can ever separate us from God's love. He promises to love us forever.

Think of a time when you were convinced that what you did or said was so bad that nobody would ever love you again. What happened? Isn't it comforting to know that, no matter what, God will always love you?

Let's Pray . . .

Dear God,
Thank you for loving us all the time, no matter what we do or say. Please help us remember to share your love with others, as we remember that we will never lose your love. Amen.

Let's Act . . .

- It's Play-Doh time!

  1. Get out a variety of colors of Play-Doh and give a different color to each member of the family.
  2. Have each person individually form their Play-Doh into a cross.
  3. Once everyone has created their cross, have them combine their crosses and mix up all the colors to make a ball.
  4. Have everyone take a piece of the ball and notice how all of the colors are completely mixed together.
  5. Talk about how hard it would be to remove the individual colors from the ball. This is how God's love for you is! You can never remove it from your life.[1]

---

1. I got the idea for this game from the Orange resources (www.thinkorange.com).

26

HIT RESET

Because of the LORD's great love
we are not consumed,
for his compassions never fail.
They are new every morning;
great is your faithfulness.

Lamentations 3:22–23

? Let's Think about It . . .

Do you ever feel disappointed with your life? Did
you have plans that didn't work out the way you
imagined they would? Did you think you could
do something—get straight As, have a particular
kind of job, find a best friend—and that hasn't happened
yet? Do your feelings of disappointment cause you to question God and wonder about the future?

Let's Get into It . . .

We need to rely on God's direction in our lives,
not on our own discernment. It's good to create
plans and to-do lists, but we can't be married to them. Though

117

things may not go as we expected, God will never disappoint us. He truly does have our best interests in mind. Sometimes we have to reach the future to look back and appreciate the past.

Our family moved to North Carolina for a year, and it was a tough season. It could have damaged our relationship with God. Once we moved back to the West Coast after a year, it was hard to understand why we were led by God to that year in North Carolina—until one day my wife and I were talking about how her biological father came back into her life during that time and they rekindled their relationship. He played an integral part in our lives that year, which ultimately helped us move back to the West Coast. He died in November 2020, and as sad as it was, we knew we had been blessed to have that close relationship with him because of our move to North Carolina. God used even a time that felt so hard for his good purposes.

Let's Learn . . .

Don't infect today with yesterday's disappointment. You may have had a rough day or a difficult week, but you can always hit the reset button. You don't have to let yesterday's failures prevent you from moving forward into the future.

We have a limited perspective on life, but God's view is infinite. If we could see all the love that God has for us, the way he views us, and the plans he has for us, our perspective on life would radically change.

Satan wants you to feel hopeless. He wants you to lose hope in the future and give up. But don't allow him to win, because you have the overcomer on your side, and his name is Jesus. God's mercy is new every morning—not some mornings, but *every* morning. If you had a bad day at school, at work, with your friends, or with your family, you can always start fresh and trust that the Lord will help you overcome yesterday.

There is a secret sauce to help us when we get down on ourselves or want to beat ourselves up over failures in our lives. When we take our eyes off of ourselves and refocus them on God and his ultimate plan, we get rid of the burden we place on ourselves and realize it's not about us. When we focus on ourselves, we can't see what's in front of us. We lose sight of how merciful God truly is. Even when we lose faith in him, his love never changes.

Sometimes you just need a new beginning. You may need to change your work or school situation. Changing some friendships may be helpful. Having New Year's resolutions can provide a fresh start for some people. Trying something new can give you motivation, renewed energy, and a fresh desire to become more of who God is calling you to be. No matter the day, no matter your age, you can hit reset and get back on track. If others try to tell you it's not possible, that you're too young or it's too late, they have not encountered our God.

Your family may not look like other families, so don't compare yourself to other people. You can be happy in your own family setting and have full confidence that God loves you so much.

God's mercy is new every morning! When things don't go our way today, he will always be with us tomorrow, offering us a fresh start.

Let's Talk about It . . .

We serve a good God! What is God working on in your life? Do you need some new friends, a new situation, or something new to try? Remember, God's mercy is new every morning!

Let's Pray . . .

Dear God,
Thank you for being so gracious, loving, and merciful.
Help us learn not to focus on ourselves and our failures.
Help us learn to focus on you and to see how good you
are. Help us to trust that your plans for our lives are
perfect. Amen.

Let's Act . . .

- Memorize this passage from the Bible.
  It will help you remember that with God,
  you will always be strong. You can even make
  some artwork with this verse and display it in your home.

> Those who hope in the LORD
>> will renew their strength.
> They will soar on wings like eagles;
>> they will run and not grow weary,
>> they will walk and not be faint.

Isaiah 40:31

- Talk about some changes you can make in your family to help you hit reset and start fresh. If you find yourselves running late all the time, maybe you need to make a family schedule and stick to it. Maybe you need to have earlier bedtimes for everyone (including Mom and Dad) to make sure everyone gets enough sleep. Maybe you need to work on your eating habits or start exercising together as a family so you feel better physically. Maybe you need to eat dinner together as a family more often. Maybe you need to pray together more consistently. Figure out the changes you need to make, and then work to make them happen!

27

CHRISTMAS

All this took place to fulfill what the Lord had said through the prophet: "The virgin will conceive and give birth to a son, and they will call him Immanuel" (which means "God with us").

Matthew 1:22–23

? Let's Think about It . . .

What is your favorite part of Christmas? Do you know why we celebrate Christmas? Is it all about Santa and receiving gifts? How is Christmas connected with the story of Jesus?

Let's Get into It . . .

Our family loves Christmastime. We love the feel of the season, the decorating, the music, blessing others with gifts, all the cool stories associated with Christmas, and, most importantly the opportunity to celebrate Jesus. Before our family opens gifts, I read the Christmas story from Luke 2. I recommend reading the Christmas story right out of the Bible so you and your family will understand the true story of Jesus' birth.

Let's Learn . . .

The Christmas story is a beautifully illustrated example of humility. The way Jesus came into this world would not have been considered a beautiful birth to most, and yet it was the most impactful event ever to take place in history.

Never has a baby been conceived in the manner Jesus was. It all started when an angel told Mary that God was pleased with her. Mary was confused and had a lot of questions swirling around in her head, but she trusted God. And God placed baby Jesus in Mary's belly. Mary was engaged to Joseph at the time, and when Joseph heard the news, he was shocked and worried. In fact, he was not sure if he should still marry her. But then an angel appeared to Joseph in a dream and told him not to be scared. The angel said that Mary had been chosen by God and that Joseph should still marry her. So he did.

That was a powerful moment of trust in God. Joseph and a pregnant Mary traveled from Nazareth to Bethlehem, a trip of about ninety miles. Can I remind you that they did not have cars during those times? You either walked or rode in a cart pulled by an animal. The Bible actually does not say that Mary traveled by donkey or some other animal. It just says, "So Joseph also went up from the town of Nazareth in Galilee to Judea, to Bethlehem the town of David, because he belonged to the house and line of David. He went there to register with Mary, who was pledged to be married to him and was expecting a child" (Luke 2:4–5). It's quite likely that Joseph and Mary walked.

This journey took them approximately four to five days. Once they arrived in Bethlehem and found a place to stay, Jesus was born. He was wrapped in cloths and placed in a manger. I'm not sure if you know what a manger looks like, but it's a long, open box or trough for animals to eat from. Mary and Joseph had to put Jesus in a manger because there were no guest rooms available in the town.

Shepherds nearby were startled by the shining of the glory of the Lord and an angel announcing the good news of a very special event. The angel said something like this: "Don't freak out, but if you go into David's town, you will find our Savior. The sign will be clear—when you find a baby wrapped in cloths and lying in a manger, when you see that little guy, you will know he is the Savior, the Messiah, the Lord!"

Without the birth of Jesus, we would not have the chance to trust in Jesus and look forward to eternal life in heaven. This is why we celebrate the birth of Jesus Christ every Christmas.

Christmas is about Jesus! On Christmas, we celebrate the greatest gift anyone has ever received—God's gift of his Son, Jesus Christ, to the world.

Let's Talk about It . . .

What does Christmas mean to you? Does your family have Christmas traditions that celebrate the birth of Jesus? How would you like to make this holiday more meaningful?

Dear God,
Thank you for loving us so much that you would
send Jesus, your only Son, into this world to save
us. Thank you that through Jesus, you give us the
opportunity to choose life in you so we can carry out
the mission of sharing your good news and one day
joining you in heaven. Amen.

Let's Act . . .

Think about some new family traditions you
would like to adopt for your family, new ways to
celebrate Jesus. Talk about some things you can do now to prepare for Christmas, even if it's months away. Some of the fun is
definitely in the anticipation!

Some of our family Christmas traditions consist of the
following:

- We like to go to the Christmas Eve service at our local
  church where we worship, sing carols, and listen to the
  pastor tell the story of Jesus' birth. Then we have our
  favorite fast food or pizza for dinner, eat a special dessert,
  and then have the kids go to bed early.
- On Christmas morning, we like to get up earlier than usual
  and get the Christmas music blaring and gather around a
  fireplace. (For a few years, I streamed the Netflix version
  of a fireplace with burning logs. Just as good, but without
  the heat.) We read the Christmas story to remind all of us
  about the reason for the season, then pray and begin to
  open presents.

28

KINDNESS IS GODLINESS

> Love is patient, love is kind. It does not envy, it does not boast, it is not proud.
>
> **1 Corinthians 13:4**

? Let's Think about It . . .

Do you ever struggle with being kind to others? How do you feel when someone is kind to you? How do you feel when someone is unkind to you? What are some characteristics of a kind person? What are some characteristics of an unkind person?

Let's Get into It . . .

When our family lived in Ventura, California, we had a nanny named Rachel who became family to us. Rachel was unbelievably selfless and kind, and our kids loved her so much. Our daughters even called Rachel their sister. I would not have been surprised if our son had a toddler crush on her, with those dreams shattered by one invitation—to Rachel's wedding.

Our family had moved to Seattle, so we had to find flights back to Ventura because we were not going to miss Rachel's wedding. We had spent about eight years living in Ventura, so on this special, but quick trip, we aimed to see as many people as possible. There was one family we wanted to make sure we saw—our neighbors from the neighborhood we lived in when Rachel was our nanny. We had only known this family for about a year, but there was a special bond between our families.

We stopped by their house and hung out for a while, and my son had brought a few of his Marvel action figures to play with their son. We did not know at the time that our son had other plans for the action figures. After our families had spent time together and were starting to say our goodbyes, Andy II gave his Iron Man action figure to his friend and said, "It's for you to keep." Honestly, we were shocked because we knew how much the Iron Man action figure meant to him.

We asked Andy, "Are you sure?" (You know how kids can be sometimes. They can give you something and then want it back a few minutes later.) He said yes. It had been his intention to give it to his friend the entire time. I love how selfless Andy was in this moment. It reminds me of today's Scripture verse where Paul speaks of selfless love and kindness modeled after God's love. God's love is so different from ours. We tend to love with conditions. If you hurt us, make us mad, or treat us dreadfully, our love changes. But God loves without conditions. His love is selfless.

Let's Learn . . .

God's love and kindness are demonstrated by us through actions of love toward others— even toward those who mistreat us. Showing love and kindness to people who aren't nice to you is godly. Being patient with people who gossip or talk badly about you is godly. Loving people when they say mean words to you is godly. Texting a friend to check up on them when you sense they are going through a tough time is godly. Helping a kid who may be hurt on the playground is godly. This godly type of love is called *agape* love, and the Bible defines it as a pure, sacrificial love that puts others before yourself.

God's love toward us is *agape*. He doesn't need anything in return from us. We are to treat others with this type of godly love. It's not an easy task; yet it is a good reminder of how God demonstrates his love for us and how we should love one another.

When Andy gave his friend his Iron Man action figure, he wasn't expecting anything in return. One day, I got a text from the boy's dad, asking for our address and telling me he had something for my son. He said his son still talks about how Andy gave him Iron Man, and he wanted to share the love. A few days later, we got a package in the mail. Their family had blessed our whole family with gifts. Like Andy's gift, this was a selfless act of love. Just like the love God has for us.

> God wants us to be kind. The Bible says, "Love is patient, love is kind." We know that God is love, so we also know that God is kindness!

Let's Talk about It . . .

Have you seen *agape* love—no strings attached and no hidden motives—shown to you or someone you know? How do you think that brought joy to the receiver? To the giver? What first step can you take to start loving others like God loves you?

Dear God,
Thank you for your overwhelming, selfless love.
Please help us to love others in the same way, so
your love for us will be seen by all. Amen.

Let's Act . . .

- Challenge one another to love people differently this week. As a family project, consider making little note cards with "Love is kind" (with all the embellishments, of course) as a reminder throughout the week. Pay close attention to how you treat your family, your friends, and even people you usually don't get along with so well. Think about what *agape* love is all about, and remember it as you interact with people this week. After the week is over, come together to share about what happened and what you learned about what it means to love.

- Who are some people around you who need to be loved? Maybe a friend or family member is having a hard time. Maybe you have a grumpy neighbor who needs to be shown love. Maybe you have some people in your life—teachers, coaches, volunteer helpers—who do a lot for others but don't seem to get a lot in return. Surprise them with loving acts—a gift card to their favorite place, a flower delivery, a plate of cookies. You don't even have to let them know who gave them the gift! Practice sharing God's love without expecting anything in return.

29

BE HEALED

Is anyone among you sick? Let them call the elders of the church to pray over them and anoint them with oil in the name of the Lord.

James 5:14

Let's Think about It . . .

Are you dealing with an illness, pain, or hurt that needs healing? Does something in your body need to be healed? Do you have a broken relationship that needs to be healed? Can your family be used by God to pray for healing for someone else?

Let's Get into It . . .

My son came home from school one day and told me about a kid in his class who was throwing up all over their books and all over the teacher during reading time. One of my daughters told me about her friend at school who has been very sad and not feeling well because her parents are going through a divorce. One of my clients at work recently was diagnosed with an illness and will need to take time off work to tend to it. All of these issues are painful to deal with if we're all alone.

Let's Learn . . .

Our world has been experiencing so much pain and turmoil, and it can be really hard to deal with. It's tough to watch the news on television or to see clips on social media because it reminds us of all the hardships and realities of life. Sometimes these reminders are triggers for the things we are dealing with ourselves.

Are you a single parent who is heartbroken? Is your family dealing with situations or relationships that are causing serious stress? Have you recently been given news about your health that is scary or serious enough to need medical attention? Kids, do you have an injury or an owie that's bothering you? Are you feeling sad about how you have been treated at home, at school, in church, on your sports team, in cheer, at dance, or in your neighborhood? If so, you don't have to suffer alone or not talk to anyone about your pain or sickness. You don't have to pray alone.

In today's Bible verse, James is speaking to those who are sick. The particular meaning of the Greek word for *sick* is "weak." Weakness has so many different looks, ranging from mental anguish to physical pain and from grief to many other issues. Sometimes you feel so weak you don't even have the strength to pray on your own, and that is okay. There is nothing wrong with admitting that you are struggling and that you or your family needs help. If this is the case, reach out to your local church or some Christian leaders you know to pray for you and your family. There is so much power when we pray over each other!

We should always be ready to pray for others who are in

need. Kids, I want you to get comfortable with asking your parents to pray for you. This opens the lines of communication so you can hear the hearts of the people in your home. This type of communication leads to stronger relationships with each other. Sometimes you may not know what the people in your home are dealing with until they ask you to pray about their specific situation or when they start praying about it during family prayer time. Parents, I want to challenge you to pray over your kids and your spouse consistently.

If you are wondering if you should use oil when you pray (as today's Bible verse talks about), that is your decision. Oil was used in this context in James to go along with prayer as a physical act that expresses a spiritual truth. It declares that we belong to God and that we rely on him, believe that he has power to comfort and heal, and trust his plan for our lives.

I urge you to share your pain with others and not try to deal with difficulties on your own. Have spiritual leaders pray over you if you need it, and always pray together as a family. Prayer heals!

God has the power to heal us—physically, emotionally, and spiritually. It is important for believers to pray for healing.

Let's Talk about It . . .

When you know that someone is hurting or going through a tough time, how can prayer help? What steps can your family take to know each other better so you can pray for healing over one another?

Let's Pray . . .

Dear God,
Thank you for hearing our prayers. Thank you that
we can call on others to pray for us when we are feel-
ing weak or down. You promise to hear our prayers!
Amen.

Let's Act . . .

- Take time together as a family to ask each other what you need prayer for. Remember that there isn't anything too small to pray about! My kids ask for prayer for their little scratches and owies all the time. This helps build their faith. Once everyone has shared their requests, take turns this week praying over each other. Praying together can be freeing and life-changing for families.

- Sometimes you may want to pray about something but then you forget all about it. Create a family prayer book in which you write down the things you are praying about— your grandpa who is having surgery, your kitty who isn't eating her food, a friend who has been crying a lot, your family car that broke down, and so forth. Be sure to write down how God answered each prayer, and to regularly look back and see how God has worked through each situation.

30

OUR IDENTITY IS IN CHRIST

You were once darkness, but now you are light in the Lord. Live as children of light.

Ephesians 5:8

? Let's Think about It . . .

Do you feel pressure to fit in with a certain group—kids at school, people at work, a group at church, individuals on a team or at a regular activity, even your best friends? Do you feel like you have to look or act a certain way to be accepted by others? Do you have a social media presence that defines who you are, and do you feel pressure to keep that up? Do you feel like you have to be "known" as something—like the funny one, the artsy one, the smart one, the athletic one? How do you imagine people see you?

Let's Get into It . . .

When I was playing college football, it was my life. Yes, I had friends, school, Bible study, parties, and my fraternity. But nothing compared to the mental and physical demands of being a full-time athlete. Being on an athletic scholarship was a different beast. Many people thought we were privileged jocks who walked around campus as if we owned it. To some degree, people were right, because if you have a cocky team member misrepresenting the team, the whole team seems guilty by association.

I started playing football when I was six years old. The game taught me so much about life and has opened amazing doors and given me incredible experiences, while also handing me injuries and identity issues. However, when the time came to check in my cleats and leave the game of football, I felt as if something was missing. I knew God told me I was done. I just didn't realize who I belonged to was more important than who I thought I was.

Let's Learn . . .

Who was I without football? I was no longer the running back on the football team. I was Andy Dooley, who had graduated from college and moved to San Diego to figure out what was next. At some point, I had lost my true identity in Christ. Going to church, attending Bible study, reading the Bible sparingly, and saying you're a Christian—those things are not enough. If we read the Bible but don't apply what it says, we are missing out on the life God has for us. When we live in this world without Jesus in our lives, we live in darkness and become vulnerable to the world's pull toward sin.

Kids, you are still growing and learning about yourself. This is a beautiful journey to be on, but you can save yourself from heartache and identity issues if you start learning early what God says about you.

When we give our lives to Christ and follow him, we become lights in a world of darkness. Jesus is the light of the world and as his followers, we are to mirror that light. Our lights are not to be extinguished by the ways of our earthly culture. Our identity is not defined by the ways of the world. Our true identity is in how God sees us. As a follower of Christ, you have been adopted into God's kingdom and you are his child.

I hope you understand you are not what other people say you are. People have a finite perspective. Some people take a snapshot of who they think you are and throw an identity label on you and box you in, without knowing the full story of who you are and the gifts you possess. You are God's creation, and what he says about you is true. Whenever you need to be reminded of who you truly are, open your Bible, read what God says about your identity in Christ, believe it, accept it, and then apply it to your life.

> **God tells us our identity is found in Christ, which is the only identity that should matter to us. What God thinks of us—that's who we are!**

Let's Talk about It . . .

How do you describe yourself? How do other people describe you? How does God describe you? When you aren't feeling confident in who you are, how can you remind yourself of your true identity in Christ?

Dear God,
Thank you that we don't have to work to gain your
acceptance. You have created us to be exactly who
we are. Amen.

Let's Act . . .

- The hardest thing to do is to accept the love of Christ and believe that what God says about you is true. Have everyone in the family write down a few things that God says about us. If you have little ones who can't write yet, choose three items from the list and have someone else write them down for the little ones to repeat. Once each person in the family has about three or four declarations listed individually, stand in front of a mirror and read the declarations out loud to yourselves. When you are done, look at yourself and say, *I believe.*

- Look at the list below and search Scripture to see where God declares each truth about our identity. Choose the one that speaks to each family member the most and create a note card for each person to display this truth in a visible place as a reminder.
  - You are chosen.
  - You are a citizen of heaven.
  - You are an heir.
  - You are forgiven.
  - You are set free.
  - You are blessed.
  - You are an indispensable part of the body of Christ.

- You are fearfully and wonderfully made.
- You are loved.
- You are a beautiful child of God.
- You are someone God takes great delight in.
- You are the salt of the earth. You bring the flavor!
- You are built different.
- You are set apart.
- You are redeemed.
- You are *one* in Christ.

31

WHY NOT US?

> It is God who works in you to will and to act in order to fulfill his good purpose.
>
> **Philippians 2:13**

Let's Think about It . . .

Would you like to be used by God? Did you know that when it comes to being used by God, it's not your age that matters? Your heart and your willingness are what matters. Would you like God to use you and your family to help change lives?

Let's Get into It . . .

The Bible is filled with the stories of people who did not seem worthy to be representatives of Jesus Christ, let alone be used by God to make lasting changes in other people's lives. Jonah tried to run from God and the calling on his life, but he could not outrun God. Moses was worried about his weaknesses and insecurities, feeling like he was not good enough, smart enough, or experienced enough. And he compared himself to others he thought were better than him.

But Moses was the one who led the Israelites out of slavery in Egypt and took them toward the promised land.
He also wrote the Ten Commandments.

Let's Learn . . .

Many things can hold us back from being used by God and missing out on blessings. But imagine what God could use you for if you would open up your hands to him and tell him, "I am willing to be used by you." What would happen if you didn't let your past and present insecurities get in the way of being used by God?

We are supposed to value ourselves the way God values us. When we devalue ourselves, we limit our progress and potential. It's easy to devalue ourselves because we see ourselves through our own limited eyes. When we learn that life is not all about us—that instead it's about Jesus and how he sees us—then barriers and walls start to fall down. And when that happens, we can better see ourselves the way God sees us and start to get a glimpse of his call on our lives as well as his ultimate plan for us.

God wants to use you. This statement should bring you so much joy, appreciation, and excitement. God wants you to take your own hands off the steering wheel of life and let him drive. The best seat in the vehicle is next to God, and you need to trust him to take you to your destination.

God wants to work in you, but first you need to decide if you are going to live for yourself or for him. Making this decision is far from easy, but the reward is so great. Letting God lead your life will challenge you, stretch you, strengthen you, grow you, save you from bad situations, keep you out of trouble, put you in good places, connect you with good people, and allow you to do things you could never imagine doing or never thought yourself capable of doing.

We may have to give up certain friendships that are not good for our growth. We may have to change our standards. We may have to make sacrifices in life. However, if we are willing to let God work according to his good purpose in us, we will have no regrets. The best way we can lead others is by letting ourselves be led by God. He is the perfect one to lead us because we can always trust him with our lives, our decisions, and our future. The books of our lives have been written, and God is the author, not us. If we allow God to guide us through life, we will be used in amazing ways for him.

God wants to use us. If our hearts are willing, that is all he needs to use us in order to help accomplish his purposes.

Let's Talk about It . . .

Are you feeling more confident about God's ability to use you? What things hold you back from allowing God to use you? Not feeling worthy? Not understanding who you are in Christ? Guilt over past sins? Insecurities about the future? How can we grow to understand God's good heart and our need to be willing to allow him to use us as he thinks best?

Let's Pray . . .

Dear God,
Deciding to turn our lives over to you sounds scary at first. We bring you all of our doubts and insecurities. Help us to believe you always have the best for us, and help us to agree to be used by you. Amen.

- Gather together as a family and ask each person this question: What areas in your life have you not fully surrendered to God? After you have taken time to think about your answer, share it with everyone and pray that you can fully surrender your life to God so he can use you to accomplish good things.

- You probably won't want to play this game for long, but maybe you can try it for part of the day (or even for just an hour). Whenever someone asks you to do something, say, "Yes, I will do that"—and then do it. (Make sure you set guidelines and aren't doing anything wrong or dangerous!) The requests may be something like washing the dishes, bringing your brother a dish of ice cream, taking the dog for a walk, doing your homework, or having a good attitude—say yes to those things. (Parents, you can play the game too. Kids, you are going to have fun with your parents saying yes all the time!) When you're done playing the game, talk about how things went. How hard was it to keep saying yes? How did it make you feel? How can you apply what you learned in this game to what God expects of you when he asks you to do something?

32

BLOOD, WATER, JESUS

One who has unreliable friends soon
comes to ruin,
but there is a friend who sticks
closer than a brother.

Proverbs 18:24

? Let's Think about It . . .

Have you ever had a friend hurt your feelings?
Have you ever had someone want to be your
friend one minute and then the next minute
they are hanging out with someone else? Do you
sometimes fight or disagree with your friends? Have you
ever had a friend betray your trust? Do you sometimes feel
alone, like you don't have any friends?

Let's Get into It . . .

In the Marvel movie *Spider-Man: No Way Home*,
the character MJ said something that has stuck

with me: "If you expect disappointment, then you can never really get disappointed." I truly believe some people live by this quote. In fact, at times I have been a victim of this mindset. I call it the lack-of-faith filter. When we can't see how a situation is going to work out and we're worried that thing won't go the way we want them to, we can try to protect our hearts from disappointment by expecting the worst, but still hope to be surprised by something better.

Let's Learn . . .

It just may be in your best interest if God closes a door you wanted to swing open. It can be better for you if by closing the door, God is protecting you from people who may enter disguised as friends but turn out to be poison. It may be in your favor that God puts distance between you and some of the people in your life. When you can fully trust God with your life, you will have a different perspective on the situations and relationships in your life.

Families can look different all over the world. In certain societies, people who are bonded through blood are assumed to be more trustworthy and loyal. But this is not always the case. Sometimes the friends we choose to have in our lives become family to us, and they are actually more trustworthy and loyal than our blood family. However, we are all human, and we are not God. We all make mistakes, disappoint one another, and hurt one another at times. A lot of the time when we hurt our family and friends, it's not on purpose. However, hurt still leaves us feeling angry, anxious, apprehensive, and alone.

God does not want us to feel alone. We were made for community, and we need human interaction with each other. It feels good to have a lot of friends. But today's verse provides a healthy warning: "One who has unreliable friends soon comes to ruin." Proverbs 18:24 isn't telling us we shouldn't have a lot of friends. We must just pay attention to whom we call family and friends. Are they there for our benefit or for their own benefit? When you experience tough times and are not thought of as popular, cool, or fun to be around, do your friends stick around and stay in touch, or do they move on to the next person?

If your foundational relationship is with the one who sticks closer than a brother, you will never be alone. God will always have your back. I can't promise that your feelings will never be hurt by other kids, brothers or sisters, friends, coworkers, people online, or anyone you may call friends or family. But there is an almighty God who loves you with compassion, concern, and care. His name is Jesus, and your friendship with him is even thicker than blood or water.

> The Bible tells us that God "sticks closer than a brother." He will be even closer to you than your best friend or closest family member. God is a friend who is always there for you and will always love you.

Let's Talk about It . . .

Is it wrong to try to protect your heart from disappointment? Is God greater than the disappointments and the people who let us down? How can you build on your relationship with God so that you learn to trust him more and lean on him?

Let's Pray . . .

Dear God,
Thank you so much for your love for us. Please protect
our friendships and our hearts. Send the right people
into our lives who will build us up and not tear us down.
Thank you for showing us your unconditional love. Amen.

Let's Act . . .

- Have a family conversation about friendship. Ask each other these questions: Who are your friends? Why do you consider them to be friends? Can you give an example of how they act like your friend? Talk about what it means to be a friend. Discuss ways you can choose good friends and ways you can be a good friend.
- Choose a book to read or a movie to watch together that has friendship as an important theme.

  Here is a list of our top six family movies that deal with friendship (in no particular order):

1. *Sing 2*
2. *Trolls* (2016 movie)
3. *UP*
4. *Zootopia*
5. *Wreck-it Ralph*
6. *Big Hero 6*

33

MENTAL HEALTH

He brought me out into a
spacious place;
he rescued me because he
delighted in me.

Psalm 18:19

? Let's Think about It . . .

When was the last time someone asked you, "How are you really doing?" Do you understand the topic of mental health? What do you think it means? Mental health is talked about a lot these days, but sometimes the genuine question of how you are really doing gets drowned out in all the talk. How are you feeling? Are you overwhelmed? Do you need to take a break?

Let's Get into It . . .

Have you ever seen your parent, brother or sister, friend, classmate, or teacher feel sick? We all get sick at times. Some sicknesses require rest or medicine to help heal the person who is sick. Your mom or dad may get a cold and not feel good, but they can still cook your dinner, go to work, and take care of you. If they rest enough and eat nutritious foods and drink a lot of water, they will soon feel better.

Some people who get sick with the flu, COVID-19, or other illnesses cannot go to work, help out around the house, or even get out of bed. They may need to go to the hospital to get checked out and may need to take medicine. We're talking about physical illnesses here, but some mental illnesses work the same way. Some people with mental illnesses can still do their everyday jobs, but they may need additional help during their illness.

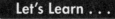

Let's Learn . . .

Regardless of our current mental state, it's important to check on our mental health often. This will require honestly sharing our feelings with others whom we trust. Depression, anxiety, loneliness, eating disorders, and many other struggles are real.

I attended a Christian convention once where one of the speakers said depression wasn't real. That statement is absolutely false. This speaker said people should pray for God to take away those feelings of depression because those feelings are not of God and the devil wants to trick us into believing we have depression. I understood the heart behind what was being said, but this message could have easily pushed people away from getting the help they needed. God has provided talented people in the mental health field who can truly help us. There is absolutely nothing wrong with getting professional help. God and others love and care about you, and you deserve to get the assistance you need to live a healthy life.

In today's Bible verse, David is talking about the tough things he has had to endure and how God's favor and grace helped save him from the enemy. David had a very close relationship with God, and he was able to speak from experience about the power of watching God work on his behalf. The closer we are to God, the more we get to experience the love and grace he has for us and the more we will see how he delivers us from tough times and tormenting situations.

When you say Psalm 18:19 out loud, let it remind you of how many times God has rescued you from a situation that seemed impossible, heartbreaking, threatening, scary, difficult, or just plain year 2020ish. God will always rescue you because he delights in you.

God cares about our mental health. He is always there to help us and bring us to a better place.

Let's Talk about It . . .

Have you ever felt so sad that you wanted to talk with someone else about it? Do you think there are people in your life you can trust enough to share those feelings with? How would you respond if someone shared with you that they were feeling sad? Who else could we direct them to if they need more help than we can give?

Let's Pray . . .

Dear God,
Thank you for promising to bring us to a place of peace and wellness. Help us reach out to others when we feel our mental health is not good. Thank you for providing people who are trained and available to help us. Amen.

Instead of including a family activity for this devotion, I want to provide a list of trusted references in case you or someone you love need professional help. Make sure to bookmark this page so you have it readily available.

988: 988 Suicide Crisis & Crisis Lifeline (24 hours a day, 7 days a week in the United States)

SAMHSA's National Helpline is available at 1-800-662-HELP (4357) or, for the deaf or hard of hearing, text them at 1-800-487-4889.

American Academy of Child and
Adolescent Psychiatry (AACAP)
3615 Wisconsin Ave. NW
Washington, DC 20016
1-800-333-7636
www.aacap.org

American Psychiatric Association (APA)
1400 K Street NW
Washington, DC 20005
202-682-6220
www.psychiatry.org/patients-families

Crisis Services Canada: 1-833-456-4566 toll-free or 1-866-277-3553 (in Quebec)

Provincial Mental Health and Addictions Crisis Line: 902-429-8167 or 1-888-429-8167 (in Nova Scotia)

Centre de prévention du suicide d'Abitibi-Ouest (Arbiti-Quest Suicide Prevention Center in Quebec): 819-339-3356 or toll-free 1-866-277-3553

13 11 14: Lifeline Australia

1800 55 1800: Kids Helpline

Anywhere in the world: www.suicide.org/international
   -suicide-hotlines.html

National Federation of Families for
Children's Mental Health
15800 Crabbs Branch Way, Suite 300
Rockville, MD 20855
240-403-1901
www.ffcmh.org

National Alliance for the Mentally Ill (NAMI)
4301 Wilson Boulevard, Suite 300
Arlington, VA 22203
1-800-950-6264
www.nami.org

Mental Health America (MHA)
500 Montgomery Street, Suite 820
Alexandria, VA 22314
1-800-969-6642
www.mhanational.org

⇒34⇐

FAITH, FAMILY, FITNESS

God said, "I give you every seed-bearing plant on the face of the whole earth and every tree that has fruit with seed in it. They will be yours for food."

Genesis 1:29

Let's Think about It . . .

Does everyone in your family feel like they get enough exercise? Is it hard to find time to work out? Kids, do you feel like you are able to get out and run around and get all your energy out every day? Do you feel like your eating habits are healthy? Do you think you eat enough fruits and vegetables? How can you grow your faith, love your family, and prioritize being healthy too?

Let's Get into It . . .

A healthy lifestyle is crucial if you want to honor the temple (that is, the body) God has given you. We are supposed to take care of the one body we get. When we abuse it by eating poorly, not working out, failing to get enough rest, or putting bad things into it, we eventually tear our bodies down. It tends to happen slowly over time, but it is inevitable if we don't prioritize a healthy lifestyle. I've worked as a fitness coach for more than thirteen years, and I've discovered that when life hits a person hard, fitness takes a back seat, but without a healthy body, we won't have energy for work, school, caring for our family, or enjoying the fruits of our labor.

Sadly, the money we are trying to save will eventually end up paying for doctor visits because of our neglected health.

Let's Learn . . .

What should our priorities be when we are trying to balance living a godly lifestyle, loving our family, and being healthy? We should start with God. God is our first love—nothing comes before him, and he is our life source. Family should come next. Parents, you have a special job to raise your children the way God intended for them to be raised. I love the way the Amplified Bible paraphrases Proverbs 22:6: "Train up a child in the way he should go [teaching him to seek God's wisdom and will for his abilities and talents], even when he is old he will not depart from it." It is the parents' job to instill in their children a love for God and his Word. This will set up our homes to have a healthy spiritual climate.

When it comes to fitness, social media platforms like Instagram, TikTok, and YouTube can be great resources to help you better yourself. A word of warning: If something sounds unfamiliar or not quite right, make sure to fact-check the information with your doctor. As a certified fitness coach, I want to emphasize that our personal nutrition has an impact on our bodies—inside *and* out. How we choose to eat will dictate how efficiently our bodies work. We can make a huge change in our bodies if we simply feed them the correct foods.

The Bible makes it a point to let us know that plants and fruits are here on this earth for us to consume. Over time, we have learned how important fruits and vegetables are for our bodies. These seed-bearing plants give us the fuel for living and reproduce themselves for generations. I'm not saying you have to adhere to a plant-based diet. I'm just saying we all need to incorporate fruits and vegetables into our daily eating.

God has given us everything we need to have a healthy physical and spiritual lifestyle that will positively impact our families and everyone we come into contact with.

> God wants every family to live a healthy lifestyle. When we take care of our bodies, we feel better and are able to do a lot more!

Let's Talk about It . . .

What steps can you take to grow closer to God, spend time together as a family, and become more fit and healthy? What tools has God given each of us to live a healthy life, both physically and spiritually. How can we make better use of them.

Let's Pray . . .

Dear God,
Thank you for creating us to be in relationship with
you and with our families. And thank you for giv-
ing us amazing bodies that can do so many things.
Please help us take good care of all the gifts you have
given us. Amen.

Let's Act . . .

- Do you want to clean up your family's eating habits? There are countless different diets and eating plans to choose from—it can be overwhelming! One good way to figure it out is to ask your doctor or another health expert which style of eating would be the best for your family in particular. Everyone is different, with different genetics and needs. However, for a well-rounded eating protocol, I suggest the Mediterranean diet due to its heart-healthy focus.

- Put together a new family schedule that prioritizes faith, family, and fitness. It starts with the "three tens":

  1. Walk together as a family or make sure you move individually for at least ten minutes a day.
  2. Read your Bible for ten minutes.
  3. Pray for ten minutes each day.

  Each week, add a minute or more to each item on the schedule. The ten minutes of each activity will become a launching pad into a healthy balance of faith, family, and fitness.

STICK AROUND

Though my father and mother
forsake me,
the LORD will receive me.

Psalm 27:10

? Let's Think about It . . .

Have you ever been abandoned by someone you love—a parent, a friend, a family member? Maybe they didn't mean to leave you alone, but it still happened. How did it make you feel? Looking back on what happened, what are your feelings about it today? Do you feel angry or sad? How has it affected your ability to trust others?

Let's Get into It . . .

I'll never forget the feeling I had when I watched the movie *Home Alone* for the first time. If you have never seen the movie, I'm sorry in advance for giving you a little bit of the plot. However, what I'm about to say will not ruin the movie for you. It will just be as if you're watching a small part of the movie trailer.

At the beginning of *Home Alone*, chaos is taking place in the McCallister household as the family is packing and preparing for a family trip to Paris. The eight-year-old son, Kevin, will not behave, so he is sent to the attic. Kevin falls asleep in the attic, and when he wakes up in the morning, he realizes that his family has already left for the airport and has accidentally left him behind at the house.

For some reason, when I watched this movie, I put myself in Kevin's shoes and felt deeply how horrible it would be to be abandoned. I had been abandoned by friends before and felt lonely. And while I'm thankful my parents never abandoned me, I know that many people have experienced abandonment and been left with feelings of pain, anger, sadness, insecurity, and resentment. If this has happened to you, I am so sorry. I want to remind you that with God in your life, you are never alone. God will always stick around.

Let's Learn . . .

In Psalm 27:10, David isn't saying his parents left him. In 1 Samuel 22:3, the Bible says, "From there David went to Mizpah in Moab and said to the king of Moab, 'Would you let my father and mother come and stay with you until I learn what God will do for me?'"

David made sure his parents were safe because he knew that no matter what was going on or would happen, God would never leave him and would take care of him. My own father grew up in a home without his biological father, which was tough for him. However, when he was a teen, he vowed to raise his own family differently. I'm thankful my father changed our family's narrative and refused to carry on a tradition of fathers abandoning their children and not being involved in their upbringing.

Kids need their parents to stick around. Parents, we need to let God be our example as we try hard to emulate his love and compassion and exercise godly leadership in our homes. We can help our children live a healthier life when we make the commitment to be a part of it. We can instill confidence, love, affection, self-worth, emotional support, and strength in our children to help them endure the rigors of school, friendships, and social settings.

The best way to learn to fight for our families is to read God's Word and learn how he fights for us. Every family needs God as their foundation. We live in a very challenging world. The enemy does not want to see us win. He knows he has already been defeated because of the sacrifice of Jesus Christ, so his full mission is to take down with him as many people as he can. We must not let him destroy more families. Stick with God and he will teach you how to stick around for your beautiful family.

> **The Bible tells us God will never leave us. He will never abandon us or turn his back on us. He is always there when we call on him.**

Let's Talk about It . . .

Now that you know a little more about abandonment, can you see how being abandoned in some way has affected your life? What can you do to form strong connections with others—especially with your family—and be there for each other, no matter what?

Let's Pray . . .

Dear God,
Thank you for loving us the way you do. Teach us to
value family as much as you do. Give us the grace to
withstand tough family moments. Give us wisdom
for navigating life's obstacles. Bless our home. And
always remind us that no matter who abandons us, you will
always be there to care for us. Amen.

Let's Act . . .

- Have a family movie night, complete
  with your favorite snacks, and watch
  Home Alone. It's a fun movie, but it also
  makes you wonder what you would do if you were in
  Kevin's shoes. Talk about what happened to Kevin and
  how you would feel in the same situation.
- The Bible has a lot to say about how God is always there
  for us and will never leave us. Look up some verses about
  God's constant love. You can write them down or memorize them so that God's promises are easy to access when
  you need them the most. It's always good to make note
  cards and set them in places where you will see them
  regularly.

=36=

OUR CALL OF DUTY

> These commandments that I give you today are to be on your hearts. Impress them on your children. Talk about them when you sit at home and when you walk along the road, when you lie down and when you get up. Tie them as symbols on your hands and bind them on your foreheads. Write them on the doorframes of your houses and on your gates.
>
> **Deuteronomy 6:6–9**

Let's Think about It . . .

Parents, do you ever wonder if you are leading your family the right way? Do you feel like you're doing a good job teaching your kids the best way to follow Jesus and live a good life? Kids, would you like to learn more about Jesus and how to be like him? Families, would you like to do a better job of having Jesus in every area of your lives so you can live for him?

Today's Scripture passage is clear and convicting and gives a vivid view of how we should approach our relationship with the Lord. When I was playing sports, whatever season I was in, I was fully immersed in that sport. If I was playing basketball, I would eat, sleep, and breathe basketball. I practiced basketball. I watched NBA and college basketball on TV. My dad and I watched basketball film on my opponents. I played basketball video games. I even carried myself as if I were a pro basketball player. I think you get it—everything revolved around basketball. Even my prayer life was focused on asking God to help me score a bunch of points, win games, and dunk the ball a couple times in each game.

Let's Learn . . .

How can we learn more about Jesus as a family, and how can we as parents learn to lead our family the godly way? We must do what Scripture says. We must make God's Word the center of our lives. We must submerge ourselves in learning about Jesus. I want this devotional to be your launching pad for a lifestyle of encountering Jesus on an everyday basis. I pray that you will be inspired to read your Bible more, pray more, study the Scriptures more, and invite the Holy Spirit into your life more.

It is important to include God's Word in our daily lives. Deuteronomy 6:6–9 says we should repeat the words of God to our children. We are to hide these powerful, life-changing Scriptures in our hearts. Imagine if the day would come when you couldn't access a Bible to read or reference. Would you have enough of the Bible memorized and hidden in your heart to help you through life? The Bible is your cheat sheet to life. Parents, you have a duty to make sure you introduce your children to the Bible and dig deeply into what the Bible says about the best way to live. The Bible is vitally important for helping us make good decisions, giving us direction, and developing our understanding of God.

We live in an intoxicating world that is flashy, distracting, and desirable to many. Parents, if we don't expose our children to the Bible, they will not have a reference point on how to live a biblically based lifestyle. I'm profoundly grateful that my parents shared the Bible with me from a young age. I can truly say that what I learned saved me from a lot of drama in college. And that's when I was listening to the Holy Spirit and not trying to be stubborn and do my own thing. But when I chose to do things my way or the world's way, I dealt with so much more heartache. I made dumb decisions and had to suffer the consequences.

Please let this Scripture passage be a turning point in your family's life. You don't have to do anything fancy. Encourage one another to fall in love with the Bible, talk about God often, listen to teachings about Jesus, read and recite the Scriptures out loud daily, memorize and hide God's Word in your heart, post Bible verses all over your house, and live a life that is pleasing to God.

> God wants to be involved in every area of our family's lives—what we do, where we go, who we interact with—anything and everything.

Let's Talk about It . . .

God wants to transform your home and your family. What are some ways your family can make God's Word a visible, active, and daily part of your home? How can you live out the Scriptures?

Let's Pray . . .

Dear God,
Thank you for giving us the ultimate life instruc-
tion manual—your Word. Help us to learn what the
Bible says about living the best life possible. Amen.

Let's Act . . .

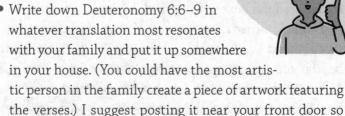

- Write down Deuteronomy 6:6–9 in
  whatever translation most resonates
  with your family and put it up somewhere
  in your house. (You could have the most artis-
  tic person in the family create a piece of artwork featuring
  the verses.) I suggest posting it near your front door so
  everyone can see it before they leave home to go out into
  the world. Jesus should be the foundation of everything in
  your life, and these verses will always remind you of that.
- Nerd out on God's Word together! Have Bible-memorizing
  competitions. Challenge each other to do a Bible study or
  read books or watch movies based on the Bible. Have fun
  learning about God's Word together.
- You can play a game I call "Bible Order":

  Write down on separate cards all the names of the
  books of the Bible. As a family, try to line them up in the
  order they are found in the Bible. Or if you like a little competition, do it in teams and see who gets the most right!
- We also play a game called "Bible Ball Toss":

  Everyone stands in a circle and says, "Genesis." The
  person with the ball tosses it to a family member, who
  has to say the next Bible book (for example, Exodus). Then
  that persons throws the ball to a family member, and the

game keeps on going to see how far you can make it without a mistake. If you know all of the books in the Bible in order, it's easier to find something you're looking for in God's Word.

37

STRONGER WITH GOD

> God chose the foolish things of the world to shame the wise; God chose the weak things of the world to shame the strong.

1 Corinthians 1:27

? Let's Think about It . . .

Do you want to be used by God? Do you feel like God can use you? Do you feel like there is anything standing in the way of your being used by God? Maybe you think you are too young. Maybe you think you don't know the Bible well enough. Maybe you think you are too busy. Maybe you think it would be better if God used someone else. Maybe . . .

Let's Get into It . . .

I went to church as a child because my parents were pastors and we kids didn't have a choice. We would go to all of the services and functions, unless we found a way to convince our parents we were sick enough to stay home. Actually, missing church was a sacrifice in many ways. Our parents knew which restaurants and stores were our favorites, and we often went to these places after church on Sundays. When we skipped church, we were sacrificing McDonald's, our favorite ice cream shop, Chinese restaurants, buffet restaurants, toy stores, the mall, and evening video games. (In our family, if you were too sick to go to church, you must be too sick to play video games. Our parents were hilarious.)

Let's Learn . . .

Back when I was a kid, if you had asked me, I would have told you I knew I was not going to be used by God. I always thought that being used by God meant you had to work in a church and be in ministry. That was not my goal in life. I didn't view myself as one of the impressive kids in the church who knew the Bible like the back of their hand. I knew I was great at sports, and I had ambitions of being a professional athlete who just happened to also be a Christian.

All the while, my wife was growing up on the opposite side of the map from me, serving in her youth group and aspiring to preach one day. But as she got older, she decided she did not want to work for a church either. She wanted to be a math teacher or run her own school one day. We didn't know each other at this point, but both of us were foolishly running from God's call on our lives.

You may be feeling like God can't use you because of your upbringing, a painful life situation, your age (thinking you're either too young or too old), personal insecurities, being hurt (maybe even by people in the church), being raised in a home where nobody believed in Jesus, or just because you think only perfect Christians can be used by God. News flash: Only Jesus is perfect, and we all fall short of the glory of God. However, all of us can be used by God right where we're at.

If you had told me I would become a pastor, youth pastor, speaker, and author, I would have eye-rolled and given you the stink eye and called you crazy—and then I would have had to repent and say, "I'm sorry, God. That was uncalled for," and go on to plead my case: "See, I'm not the one you want to use." In today's Scripture verse, Paul reminds us that God does not care how polished, perfect, or put together we are. Throughout history, God has chosen ordinary sinners to do his work—those who were despised, ignored, overlooked, and abused, and especially those humble enough to become followers of God.

Unfortunately, fame and wealth have prevented some people from believing in the one true God because they don't think they need God for anything, which is a prideful place to be. In the Bible, the Jews and the Greeks thought Jesus was a foolish weakling for dying on a cross to save us. People today think we are foolish to believe in this Jesus who was so weak that he couldn't save his own life. But they just don't understand. Not only did Jesus rise from the grave in three days, but he also defeated sin and smacked Satan in the mouth by giving all of us the opportunity to follow him and choose eternal life.

God can use anyone to further his kingdom. You don't have to be the strongest or the smartest or the most popular. You just need to be available.

Let's Talk about It . . .

Did you know there's such a thing as "strength in weakness"? It's better to follow Jesus and have the world call you weak, because there is power in weakness. Talk about how your family can follow Jesus and find strength in weakness. In what ways are you weak that God can use for his glory.

Now that you know God has no limits on who can be used by him, how are you feeling about being a part of his plan? What do you think God is asking you to do for him today?

Let's Pray . . .

Dear God,
Thank you that we don't have to be perfect to start living for you. Help us overcome our fears and insecurities and recognize that right now, we are good enough to start doing kingdom work. Amen.

Let's Act . . .

- As your family thinks about its strengths and weaknesses, have each family member share how God might use one of their weaknesses to show his glory to those around you.
- Get together as a family and have each person write down the name of a person they know who needs Jesus in their life. Have everyone in the family pray for these people every day during the week, that they would give their lives to Christ and start a new life living for Jesus.

38

FUN IS WHAT WE NEED

A cheerful heart is good medicine
but a crushed spirit dries up the bones.

Proverbs 17:22

? Let's Think about It . . .

When is the last time your family had a lot of fun together? What are some things everyone in your family likes to do for fun? The demands of the day can become overwhelming and suck the joy right out of us. How do you tend to react when this happens? Which people in the family are the fun ones, and which ones tend to be the fun police? It honestly doesn't take much to enjoy life and have fun, so start getting yourself into the "having fun" mindset.

Let's Get into It . . .

Did you know some people think that once you become a Christian, you lose your cool factor and aren't able to have fun anymore? I understand where people may get that idea. I remember looking at some older churchgoers as a kid and being so turned off by how they lived as Christians. They seemed so stiff and stuffy. I'm thankful my mom and dad knew how to have fun.

My dad was a jokester. He was so funny and slick with his trash-talking, but it had a really cool factor to it. My dad grew up on the streets, played sports, was witty, and had some natural swag. My mom is from Trinidad and was very outgoing, positive, and sweet, and she loves to have fun. The combination of who they were as parents and Christians has truly had an impact on my life. They showed me how important it is to have joy in life.

Let's Learn . . .

Joy has an effect on our health, just as much as working out, having good nutrition, taking time to relax and unwind, and getting enough sleep. In the Bible, Solomon was on to something well over three thousand years ago: A joyful heart is good medicine! There are scientific studies proving that laughter, a sense of humor, and joy can add years to our lives. If you have a choice to be happy or angry, it is in your best interest to choose happiness and joy. You need it, your kids need it, your friends need it, we all need it.

We have tried to adopt this way of life for our family. All of us will have our tough and sad days where it's hard to smile or find joy. A friend at school may hurt your feelings, parents may get in an argument when they don't see eye to eye, kids may get upset when they can't find a favorite stuffed animal or toy, adults may feel stress at work, kids may feel stress at school, a family may have lost a loved one. I understand the journey. Our family has had those difficult times too. However, we all do have a choice.

As you take the time to mourn and face the challenges, remember that God has the ability to turn a broken spirit into a joyful one. Parents, be careful how you talk to your kids when you (and they) are upset. If they need to be corrected, do it in love without breaking their spirits. Breaking a child's spirit can do lasting damage physically, mentally, and spiritually.

Parents, this part is also for you. Just because you are an adult does not mean you are immune to the trauma that words can do. Practice intentionally speaking well of others. Lift up other people with encouraging, life-giving words. Build up your beautiful kids with kind words soaked in joy. Kids, this part is for you. Tell your parents how awesome they are. Your parents need to tell you "I love you," and you need to tell them that too.

Families, find things to do together that are fun for everyone in the family. Plan family time together and also have breakout fun, where the fun isn't planned but just happens, where you make memories and grow closer as you laugh with and enjoy each other. Fun is what we need!

> God wants us to have joy in our lives, and part of that joy is having fun. Making fun memories together as a family is one of the best things you can do.

Let's Talk about It . . .

Having fun together is important, even in busy families! Does your family do a good job of making time for fun? What can you do to make fun a priority in your life?

Dear God,
You have given us so many things, and you have
also given us the gift of fun. Thank you for laughter
and giggles and joy and goofiness. Help our family
to have fun together. Amen.

Let's Act . . .

- One summer our family committed to doing one hundred push-ups a day for sixty days. We called it the push-up challenge. We rested on Sundays, and everyone participated. (Yes, even our fifteen-month-old participated, with some of the funniest versions of push-ups you will ever see! Bless her heart, she just wants to do everything we do around the house.) At the end of the sixty-eight days (it was a sixty-day challenge with eight days off), every person received money for a Target shopping trip as a reward for how many push-ups they completed.

  You can make this work for your family and your finances, but in our challenge, everyone received one dollar when they completed each day except for Andy II and Ava—the younger ones received 25 cents. Our son was still learning how to do correct push-ups, so we gave him 25 cents for each one of those attempts at push-ups. You better believe he got better at them by the end of sixty-eight days.

  Here are the results of how many days each person completed and how much money they made:

  Dad: 60 days/$60

Mom: 50 days/$50
Hope: 58 days/$58
Skylee: 58 days/$58
Andy II: 49 days/$12.25
Ava Joy: 7 days/$1.75

When we went to Target together, we all had a huge feeling of joy, accomplishment, excitement, and *fun*. Parents, your kids will always remember the family mood and how you made them feel. Kids, parents will always remember your smiles and laughter. Have fun together as a family and create memories that will last.

- Choose your own challenge for your family. You could do our family push-up challenge, or you could pick something more in line with your family's interests and hobbies. Figure out what you can work on consistently for a certain period of time and then set goals and prizes for when you reach the end of your journey. Have fun working and playing together!

39

DISCERNMENT

The fear of the LORD is the beginning
of knowledge,
but fools despise wisdom and
instruction.

Proverbs 1:7

Let's Think about It . . .

Do you know what discernment is? If so, do you
believe you have it? If not, what do you think
it means to have "discernment"? What exactly
is discernment, and where does it come from?

Let's Get into It . . .

God has guided me so many times in my decision making. There was a season before I was
married when I felt like I had to take a period of time to myself
to spend more time with God and remain single. I didn't just
choose to do this; it felt important to follow this prompting from
God. During this time, I met a lot of cool people, and some of my
friends tried to introduce me to really nice girls. However, I knew
that relationships couldn't go beyond a friendship at that point.

After many months of time alone with God, I was asked to go to the airport to pick up some pastors who were speaking at our church. Within the first five minutes of meeting them, they asked if I was single. Then they proceeded to tell me my future wife was in Seattle. I laughed it off, but at that moment I felt like God said it was okay to pursue this possibility. My obedience from months before prepared me for my future wife. They were right. Within eleven months, I began dating a girl named Tiffany—the one to whom I would get engaged and tie the knot. We just celebrated twelve years of marriage and now have four beautiful children.

Let's Learn . . .

What exactly is discernment? Discernment as defined by the Bible is the ability to make decisions and understand situations while being guided by the Holy Spirit. Having discernment simply means we can decide what is right or wrong by thinking biblically. How do we get and exercise Christian discernment? We first have to spend time with the Lord and read our Bibles. We must also ask God for spiritual wisdom, godly insight, and the ability to make good judgments.

When you read your Bible and pray, give God a chance to speak to you. And give yourself a chance to listen for God in the silence. Choose to have a dialogue with God instead of just engaging in a monologue. Trust me, God has a lot to say!

Ask God to give you discernment daily. Kids, when you pray to God with your family or by yourself, ask God to give you spiritual discernment. Ask him to help you with the decisions in your life. You are never too young to start developing discernment. Parents, having discernment should also be the desire of your hearts as you navigate your crazy, busy, distracting, and complicated days. We have many decisions to make every day, and sometimes it's hard to know what the right decision is. If you are an ambitious go-getter and don't like to wait for things, it will be in your best interest to pause for God to give you the go-ahead to act instead of zooming off on your own, only to experience a setback and start all over again.

We all have to make major decisions in our lives. Should I stay at this job? Should we move? Should I find a different group of friends? What school should the kids go to? Is this the right activity for me? Which church is the best one for our family? Some of the decisions you make in life are small and don't really matter much, but other decisions have a major impact on your future. Without God's help, you're simply guessing. There is nothing wrong with creating a plan and following it, but the Bible says in Proverbs 16:9 that "humans plan their course, but the LORD establishes their steps." When you are making decisions, always leave room for God to speak and interrupt your plans and be flexible so you can make an response when you hear God's voice.

If you don't like being told what to do and prefer to do things your own way, you have a slippery slope to navigate. Kids, when your parents give you direction and wisdom, please listen to them. When they ask you to clean your room, it's not just to make you do work. They are wanting you to form good habits, and cleanliness is one of them. If you have never been taught how to clean up after yourself, shower, brush your teeth, wash your hands, wash dishes, do laundry, or wash your hair, you may end up creating an environment where bacteria will grow and cause you to get sick.

In this world, you will be given a lot of information, and plenty of people will speak worldly "wisdom" to you. Although some of these things may sound good, spiritual discernment will help you decide if they are actually good or bad for you. Ephesians 4:13–14 says, When "we all . . . become mature, attaining to the whole measure of the fullness of Christ . . . then we will no longer be infants, tossed back and forth by the waves, and blown here and there by every wind of teaching and by the cunning and craftiness of people in their deceitful scheming." When we apply biblical discernment to our lives, we will be able to sort out what is truth from what is a lie and make the decisions God wants us to make.

God wants us to have spiritual discernment. Fortunately, we don't have to figure things out on our own. The Bible gives excellent guidance on developing a discerning spirit.

Let's Talk about It . . .

We can keep our feet firmly on the solid Rock, Christ, even if we are going through spiritual, mental, or physical trials. How can your family start to do this today?

Let's Pray . . .

Dear God,
Thank you for giving us the gift of spiritual discernment. Give us the patience to listen to you, and make our eyes, ears, and hearts sensitive to your voice. Amen.

Let's Act . . .

- As a family, make a list of all the ways the world wants us to follow it instead of God. Think of examples from your own life. Then write down the consequences of following the world instead of God. Next, write down the ways God wants us to follow him, and then the consequences of listening to God's direction. Talk about which way is the better way to live.
- Let's play the "Healthy/Unhealthy Choice" game.

Supplies needed:

- Markers
- Poster board
- Photos from newspapers, magazines, flyers, or your computer
- Tape

1. Draw a line down the middle of the poster board. Draw a thumbs-up on one side of the line and a thumbs-down on the other.
2. Have everyone cut out photos of healthy foods, junk food, and nonedible objects.
3. Have the kids decide on what is healthy to eat and tape it on the thumbs-up side; have them post what isn't healthy to eat on the thumbs-down side. Allow them to figure out what's right and what's wrong for healthy eating, which will help condition them to think about what is right and wrong in life.
4. You can do the same thing for the nonedible items they've cut out. Is a skateboard healthy or unhealthy?

A dog? A fast car? You can even discuss how sometimes it's about timing or what God wants for you in a specific season.

5. Talk about listening to what God says is good for us and for our bodies—and what it means to follow what he says.

40

WHEN YOU DON'T FIT IN

The thief comes only to steal and kill
and destroy; I have come that they
may have life, and have it to the full.

John 10:10

Let's Think about It . . .

Do you ever wonder if things you have done in the past will keep you from experiencing the goodness of God? Do you understand how God sees you? Do you know you were created *on* purpose and *for* a purpose? Do the people in your life support you and encourage you to follow God, or do they try to distract you from doing the right thing? Do you ever feel like it's really hard to be yourself?

Let's Get into It . . .

"You don't fit."

"I don't know where you fit, you just don't fit here."

179

These words were said to my face. When I heard them, everything in the room went dead silent as the words echoed around in my head as if they had been spoken in an empty basketball arena. I visualized myself coming out of my body like a ghost, picking up by the neck the person who had spoken these words, and Hulk-slamming them three times before booting them way off to Mars. I was so mad that I felt the sweat bead up on my nose, my ears get summer-in-Arizona hot, and my mouth go dry. But then I came back to reality and felt my emotions shifting from mad to sad. I started to question my worth: *Is this true? Do I not fit in anywhere? Do I not have a purpose? Am I not a leader? Am I not gifted, talented, or even worthy?*

Let's Learn . . .

So many things go through your head when you're told you don't belong. And Satan wants you to believe these lies about yourself.

- He wants you to question your purpose.
- He wants you to fail to see the beauty in yourself.
- He wants to steal your confidence.
- He wants to steal your joy.
- He wants to use your insecurities as signaling truth in your life.
- He wants you to question why you exist.
- He wants to divide families.
- He wants to turn spouses against each other.
- He wants to be so loud in your life that you can't hear the voice of God.

However, God wants entirely different things for you.

- God wants you to know Satan has already been defeated.
- God wants you to know you have a purpose.
- God wants you to know you are beautiful and handsome.
- God wants you to have confidence in him and in yourself.
- God wants you to have joy.
- God wants you to be secure in who he has created you to be.
- God wants you to live and be a part of this world.
- God wants to use your discomfort to help comfort others.
- God wants to unite families.
- God wants parents and kids to love each other.
- God wants to walk with you every step of the way.

The enemy will always try to derail you and block what God has for you, which is a life of purpose, spiritual guidance, and blessings. If you grew up in a household with pain, abuse, divorce, trauma, depression, sadness, or stress, please don't let those things define who you are. God always offers redemption. You and God together can change the narrative of your life. You can find joy and love. You can do your part to bring harmony and unity to your family. You can raise your kids to love Jesus.

Your family is worth the hard work it takes to overcome your past and become closer to each other and to God. The only way to live an abundant and fulfilling life is through Jesus. He is the key to living a fulfilling life that loosens the grip of the enemy. Don't believe the lies the world tells you; believe the truth Jesus tells you.

God wants us to live an abundant life, and his version of the best life means we fit in with him, not with the world.

Have you ever felt like you don't fit in? What lie of Satan did that tempt you to believe? Would you rather be set apart for God to use in your uniqueness? Or would you rather spend your life striving for the sameness of this world? Why?

Let's Pray . . .

Dear God,
Please help us appreciate the wonderful individuals you have created us to be. Give us strength and discernment to not believe any lies spoken over us and our lives. Help us remember that we are made in your image and made with purpose. Amen.

Let's Act . . .

- Continue the discussion you started before prayer. Have everyone talk about a specific time when they felt like they didn't fit in. What happened? Did they change who they were in order to fit in, or did they walk away and find a place where they would be more accepted? You can also discuss how our environment can make us question who we are. Do we want to change how we look or act because of pressure from our peers? How can we be content to be the person God created us to be?

- Sometimes in life you fit in just fine and it's someone else who is being excluded. Think of some people you know who don't seem to fit in. Maybe it's a classmate or a coworker who is a little bit different from everyone else. Maybe a family at your church has a disabled child and it's hard for them to connect with others. Maybe a new neighbor is having trouble getting to know other people in the neighborhood. Think of ways to help these people feel accepted as you share Christ's love with them.

41

HONOR AND RESPECT

> Be devoted to one another in love.
> Honor one another above yourselves.
>
> **Romans 12:10**

? Let's Think about It . . .

How does it make you feel when another person disrespects you? Do you always treat others with respect? Do you pay attention to other people and do what they ask you to do? Do you tend to get too comfortable with the people you are close to (like your family) and slip up on respect at times?

Let's Get into It . . .

Honor and respect come in many forms. However, one way you can show everyone, anywhere, a form of honor and respect is by being selfless. I was always taught that if you are in public and get to a door first and there are people behind you, you should make sure to open the door for them. This selfless act will always make someone feel honored or respected.

It's so cool to watch my kids try to outserve each other. My son will run to the car and wait for us to click the clicker so he can open the doors for my wife and me. We are still working on him doing it consistently for his sisters! My daughter Skylee does this for strangers in public all the time, so much so that she tries to fight me once in a while to be the one holding the door open.

Let's Learn . . .

Kids, if your parents ask you to stop running around the house, jumping on the furniture, eating on the couch, running ahead of them in public, fighting with your siblings, talking back, or staying up too late at night, do you listen? Do you take their words seriously? If you don't, you are showing them disrespect. And you are not showing your parents that you value them.

God wants you to respect everyone. If you are a believer in Jesus Christ, other believers are considered your brothers and sisters. As humans, it's natural to make mistakes and let our emotions get the best of us. And at times like these, we can be disrespectful to each other. But respecting others is important. Respect is a mirror that shows our own level of honor and respect for God. First John 4:20 says, "Whoever claims to love God yet hates a brother or sister is a liar. For whoever does not love their brother and sister, whom they have seen, cannot love God, whom they have not seen."

Ouch! This verse gets me every time because sometimes even brothers and sisters in Christ do really bad things and hurt one another's feelings. It can be hard to show respect to people who hurt us. That is why we need God daily. We can't do this on our own. Mom and Dad may get into an argument that could sound like they are being disrespectful toward each other. However, if they love God, they will ask him for forgiveness and then ask each other for forgiveness.

The Bible has a "golden rule" that says we should treat others the way we would like to be treated (Matthew 7:12). No one wants to be disrespected. We might desire deeply to be like Jesus. But we can't be like Jesus if we don't have a relationship with him. If we don't read the Bible, pray, and learn about the ways of Jesus, how are we going to know what he is like? The good news is that the words in the Bible can renew a person's heart. If we let it, God's Word can completely change us in a good way.

Romans 12:10 says, "Love one another with brotherly affection. Outdo one another in showing honor" (ESV). Wow! Imagine if we as believers in Christ aimed to outdo one another in showing honor and respect. How life-changing that would be for our relationships! When you honor someone, you show high esteem for them. If you want to be treated with respect, treat others with respect.

Parents, your kids deserve your respect. You hold a special place in their hearts, and God has entrusted you with their care. So be careful how you treat them. Kids pick up on everything we do, and our actions make more of an impact on them than we realize. When you show your kids respect in the home, you will teach them how to respect and honor other people outside the home. Make honor and respect a part of your everyday lives, and your family can help change the world!

> God wants us to treat each other with respect.
> A good rule of thumb is to remember to treat
> people the way you want to be treated.

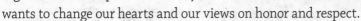

What would it look like if we changed the dynamic in our home and tried to outdo one another in showing honor and respect? How do you think Jesus wants to change our hearts and our views on honor and respect.

Let's Pray . . .

Dear God,
Thank you for modeling what it means to show honor and respect to others. Please help us treat others in the way we would like to be treated instead of putting ourselves first. Amen.

Let's Act . . .

- If anyone in your family has felt disrespected by another family member, take some time to share your feelings with one another. Your home should be a safe setting where everyone can speak honestly and nobody should feel bad or defensive. Give one another a chance to reconcile and ask for forgiveness if someone has felt disrespected. Then pray together that you will develop a desire to outdo one another in showing honor and respect.

- It's always good to say, "I'm sorry," with words, but your actions show you are sorry as well. Kids, if you have not shown respect to your parents, help them cook dinner or clean the garage or make them a special card. Parents, if you have not shown respect to your kids, make them their favorite meal, take them on a special outing, or buy them a small gift. Hugs and kisses are important too!

42

LOVE THOSE WHO DON'T LOOK LIKE YOU

The LORD said to Samuel, "Do not consider his appearance or his height, for I have rejected him. The LORD does not look at the things people look at. People look at the outward appearance, but the LORD looks at the heart."

1 Samuel 16:7

? Let's Think about It . . .

Have you ever had to deal with unfair treatment of any sort—maybe because you look different or act differently than others do? Does anyone in your family have a disability and feel like they have been treated differently because of it?

One breezy California evening, I was heading
home from work in rush hour traffic on the 101.
I was driving down a hill when I received a phone call from my
wife. "Babe," she said, "guess what? We were just given a car!" I
could not believe the news she had just shared, but it truly did
not register in my mind because the car I was driving had just
started to jerk. While I was listening to my wife on speaker-
phone, I was trying to steer my car into a truck weigh station
because the engine had suddenly stopped working.

With cars zipping by me, I was trying to time my entrance
into the weigh station so I wouldn't get hit. I'm not sure I was
even breathing while trying to do this. I knew that every second
counted, and I did not want to mess up. I finally glided into the
weigh station. Once the car stopped, everything completely shut
down. I told my wife, "Babe, this is crazy timing to be given a car
because this car just died!" You can imagine our disbelief. But
before I could even collect my thoughts, a police officer came up
behind me, flashing his lights and yelling over the loudspeaker,
"Move your car. It can't be here!"

I placed my hands on the steering wheel and waited for the
officer to approach my vehicle. Once he reached the driver's side
door and saw me, he become even more aggressive and yelled at
me again to move my car. I calmly told him, "Officer, I cannot
move my car. The engine just died. Would you mind helping
me move it?" I couldn't make this up. He kept screaming at me
while he gripped his baton and then walked back to the police
car, taking a close look at my license plate number.

My wife started to pray on the phone, and within minutes,
the officer showed up at the window of my car as if he were a
completely different person. I kid you not. I was in disbelief as he

began to help me and acted like he hadn't just been yelling at me moments before. But it still didn't take away the hurt and fear of how he had treated me—treatment that had been uncalled for and may have been based, at least in part, on my outer appearance. I am just thankful my wife started praying when she did.

Let's Learn . . .

It never feels good to be treated differently because you look or act different from others. And it's not right for people to treat us that way. God does not judge us based on our differences or disabilities. He looks at our hearts.

We are to treat people by looking at their hearts as well. Even if someone looks or acts differently than you and your friends, you should always treat them with love and respect. Everyone has differences, and each of us was created by God in our own unique way. We are not to judge people based on their appearance. A classmate, coworker, neighbor, teammate, influencer, celebrity, or anyone else can look great on the outside and say all the right things but still have dishonesty in their heart. When we judge other people based on their exterior, we are more liable to be influenced by deception. God knows our hearts, but we don't often know the hearts of our peers or even family members. We need God's help to recognize what is in the heart of a person instead of judging them based on how they look.

Just because a person may look or act differently from you does not mean you should love them any less. If you have been treated unfairly or judged by anyone, I personally want to tell you I am so sorry you have had to deal with that. I know how it feels, and I pray that God will wrap his loving arms around you and remind you that you are special to him. You are not defined by the world's standards. You are defined by God's standards, and he will always treat you as one of his dearly loved children.

God sees our hearts, and he sees how we feel about others. We need to pray for God to change our hearts so we can love everyone, including those who are not like us.

Let's Talk about It . . .

Do you find it difficult to believe that God loves you as much as he loves anyone else? How can we as a family find ways to love those who don't look like us?

Let's Pray . . .

Dear God,
Thank you for creating each of us to be different from one another—but as your children created in your image. Remind us when we see someone who is not like us that they are loved by you. Please help us love others, no matter how similar to or different from us they are. Amen.

Let's Act . . .

- Grab some lunch-sized paper bags for each member of the family. Allow each person to decorate the bag in whatever way they want, using markers, pens, stickers, paint, or any other creative supply you have in your home. The outside decorations can represent what is inside the bag or can be completely different from what's inside. Next, choose an object you can find around the house—a rock, a pen, some coins, a toy, a spoon, an apple—that will fit inside the bag. (Don't show anyone else the item!) After everyone has secretly put an item inside their bag, take turns guessing what is in each bag based on the decorations on the outside of the bag. Once you have made your guesses, each person can reveal what's inside their bag. Remember, what is on the outside does not always represent what is on the inside. Talk about how this can be a reminder that only God knows people's hearts, but no matter what's in a person's heart, we should love them as someone created in God's image!

- Consider reading one or more of these books (or watching the movie) that our family likes on this topic:

1. *We Are Family* by LeBron James and Andrea Williams
2. *I Am Enough* by Grace Byers
3. *All Are Welcome* by Alexandra Penfold
4. *The Day You Begin* by Jacqueline Woodson
5. The movie *Hidden Figures*

43

BUSY, BUSY, BUSY

> Do not wear yourself out to get rich;
> do not trust your own cleverness.
>
> **Proverbs 23:4**

Let's Think about It . . .

Kids, do you ever wish you could spend more time with your parents? Does it seem like they are always working or busy doing other things? Of course it's important for parents to work and to have hobbies—they need to provide for you and take care of you and find joy in what they like to do. But they also really want to spend time with you. Parents, do you often feel overworked and tired? Are you motivated to work long hours because you are trying to reach certain goals—make more money, build your business, have more financial freedom? But are you so busy working that you're spending less and less time with your family?

Let's Get into It . . .

The world we live in can suck the life out of us if we let it. We need to be able to set boundaries for ourselves, and parents, you need to set a good example in this for your kids. I once worked for a company that told us to our face in a new hire orientation, "If you let us, we will work you as much as possible." I remember typing that quote into my iPad.

After orientation, I went up to the presenter and asked, "What did you mean when you said, 'If you let us, we will work you as much as possible'?" The presenter replied that the company would take advantage of anyone who didn't come into the job with boundaries already in place. They would work you until you burned out and quit, and then they would replace you with someone else. I asked him, "Why are you still here?" He said, "I have boundaries for balance in my life. If those are ever compromised, I will no longer stay." That stuck with me. I made it clear to the company from that day forward that my relationship with God came first, then my family, and then work. If the company could not respect my boundaries, it would not be the place for me.

Let's Learn . . .

I'm ambitious, and I want to provide for my family. Not working to reach my goals isn't an option. However, I tend to get so wrapped up in achieving my goals, working to build more provision for our family, and become so busy that my personal time with God—along with time with my family—can take a back seat to my work. This is completely backward in God's sight. And when we let work or anything else come before God and family, Satan uses that busyness to harm our relationship with God, our relationship with our families, and our purpose on earth.

Satan would love to trick us into thinking we have to work endlessly, make lots of money, and be successful. It's easy to become consumed by our own personal goals and believe we can do it all without God. Kids, your parents love you so much and want to provide for you. The desire to work hard is an awesome attribute to have. The food you eat, the roof over your head, the toys you play with, and the clothes you wear all come from the hard-earned money your parents have worked to make. But your parents also need to spend time with God and with you.

Parents, we can't just mix up our priorities or do it all on our own. God should always come first, and what he can do while you exercise balance in your life will blow your mind. God opens doors no person can shut, and he shuts doors no person can open. God does not want you to be exhausted, weak, and absent from your family. He wants to spend time with you and wants you to spend time with your family. Do you realize that in this broken world we could lose all our savings in a moment? Then where would you be? Have you fostered your relationships with God and with your family so that you have their support to help you through tough times like that?

Do you realize that with a snap of God's fingers, all of your finances could be gone? Then you would be without God, without your family, and without your finances—a really tough place to be.

Here are some things I believe God wants for you:

- God wants you to have your priorities in order.
- God wants to work on your behalf.
- God wants to spend time with you.
- God wants to share his heart with you.
- God wants you to have a strong family life.
- God wants you to be healthy.
- God wants to bless you.

God wants us to have a healthy balance of spending time with him, spending time with our families, and spending time at work and on other important things.

Let's Talk about It . . .

How do you think we are balancing our time with God, family, and work (or school for the kids)? Do we need to come together as a family and figure out how to rethink our priorities?

Let's Pray . . .

Dear God,
Please help our family learn to balance time with you, with one another, and with work, school, or other commitments. Amen.

Let's Act . . .

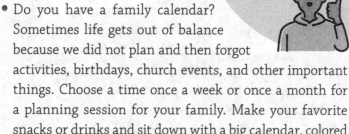

- Do you have a family calendar? Sometimes life gets out of balance because we did not plan and then forgot activities, birthdays, church events, and other important things. Choose a time once a week or once a month for a planning session for your family. Make your favorite snacks or drinks and sit down with a big calendar, colored pens, and your phones or laptops so you can look up different events and activities. Write down the big things on the family calendar—the trip to Disney, sports games, band concerts, school events, birthdays, holidays, camping trips, church camps, and so forth. Hang the calendar where everyone will see it and check it before they add anything else to the schedule.

- We do a couple other things to keep our lives and priorities in balance: (1) make sure to pray with each other every night before bed and (2) have a Friday Family Fun Night as often as possible, where we watch a movie together. Though these are little things, they remind us to put what's really important first in our lives and on our schedule. Discuss what your family can do to keep your lives and priorities in balance.

⇒44⇐

TECHNOLOGY TODAY

Through him [Jesus] all things were made; without him nothing was made that has been made.

John 1:3

? Let's Think about It . . .

How does everyone in the family feel about the use of technology in your home? Parents, do you think that cell phones, tablets, computers, and video games take away from family time? Kids, do you have video games, a tablet, a computer, Netflix, Disney+, or a way of streaming videos from the multiple platforms that exist? How much does your family use social media? Do family members have a limit on how much technology they use and how much time they spend on devices?

Let's Get into It . . .

We love and appreciate technology in our home. We enjoy using tablets and gaming systems.

However, my wife and I set limits on how much time is spent in front of a television or on tablets. During Christmas, we surprised the older kids with tablets at the very end of our gift giving. I set up a scavenger hunt that led to them finding electronic tablets underneath their pillows. During the holiday break, we were lenient with their usage. However, now that school has started back up, they can only play on them if their homework is done and they have done their chores, and then it's only for thirty minutes. If they have an attitude when we tell them to stop and put them away, they lose the privilege for the next day.

Let's Learn . . .

We are surrounded by so much evolving technology today. By the time you read this devotion, there will be more new groundbreaking technology, new devices, new streaming platforms, and new real estate in the metaverse than there was when I wrote this book. Some people love the technology evolution, and some people cannot stand it. The simple truth is, we were all created by God to be different—and some of us were created to become creators! Consider some examples:

- Ada Lovelace, an English mathematician from the 1800s who was considered to be the first computer programmer, was created by God.
- Steve Jobs, who cofounded Apple Computer, Inc.—famous for the iPhone, the iPad, and more—was created by God.
- Douglas Engelbart, who alongside his lead engineer invented the computer mouse, was created by God.
- Gerald Anderson Lawson, who designed the Fairchild Channel F video game console and helped lead the creation

of a commercial video game cartridge, was created by God. (Lawson's vision sparked the beginnings of the major consoles we know and love today, from Atari 2600 to Nintendo, Sega Master System, PlayStation, Xbox, and more.)

- Nathaniel Borenstein, the email pioneer, was created by God.
- Carol Shaw, famous for being the first female video game designer—her creations include Atari 3D Tic-Tac-Toe—was created by God.

Kids, you could become the next designer, programmer, engineer, mathematician, or creator of the next big wave of technology. You never know. All of us were created by God with a purpose to fulfill. And all of God's creation is good. So much controversy surrounding technology today exists not because it was created but because so many people misuse it. In many cases, devices have prevented us from establishing relationships with other people. But phones, tablets, TVs, and computers don't divide our homes; *we* divide our homes. Blaming Instagram, Facebook, TikTok, YouTube, or other social media outlets for the time taken away from each other is not fair. You—not social media—are the ones who control your household.

We don't always like it, but we all need to have structure. Without it, the world can be a scary place. Without structure, we tend to flounder around aimlessly. Creation has a structure to it. None of us were created by accident. The gifts and talents we all possess were given to us by God. How we use them will affect our world for good or for bad, which is why people consistently struggle with certain gifts that have been used by the devil or used for worldly gain. When we need help with life's challenges, direction, and purpose, we must connect with our Creator for his guidance and fundamental focus. He will help us navigate through everything, including the technology issues we face today.

God has created everything that has created other things. So technically, God has created technology! He wants us to use it—and everything he has created—wisely.

Let's Talk about It . . .

What are some ways that technology can be used for good? Do you think we ever allow it to become a substitute for spending time with God, our families, and other people? Since it's very easy to become addicted to many forms of technology, how can we set limits and constantly evaluate how and how much we use it?

Let's Pray . . .

Dear God,
Thank you for the gift of technology and all the cool things we can do with it. Please help us use our time wisely and know when it is time to stop using devices and connect with you and others in person. Amen.

Let's Act . . .

• Parents, this one is for you. You have the opportunity to control the technology thermostat in your home.

Create constraints around device use at home. When you all sit down for family time to read the Bible and a devotion, make sure all devices are put away. (You can do this in other situations too, like at meals or when people come over to visit.) Establish a limit to the use of gaming consoles, video streaming, internet browsing, TV watching, and handheld games. You know what is best for your family. If you don't know exactly what limits your family needs, you will soon figure it out through trial and error.

- Kids, take a look at how much you use technology. If you would rather text a friend than hang out with them in person, you need to reevaluate things. Texting is fun, but it's no substitute for having fun together. Memories aren't made through text messages. Keep a diary of how much time you spend on screens throughout the day. The number of hours might shock you! (Parents, you can do this right along with your kids.) As a family, make a list of fun nonscreen activities. Here are a few we like:

  - read a book
  - play with the dog
  - make crafts
  - play a board game
  - bake cookies
  - go outside and shoot hoops
  - draw a picture
  - go to the park and play Frisbee

Make your own list and post it somewhere in your home so family members can find something to do when they've run out of screen time!

45

THE THIRST IS REAL

> Whoever drinks the water I give them will never thirst. Indeed, the water I give them will become in them a spring of water welling up to eternal life.
>
> **John 4:14**

Let's Think about It . . .

Have you ever been playing outside on a hot summer day and got really thirsty? Or have you been doing a hard workout at the gym and discovered you forgot your water bottle? How did you feel when you were finally able to drink some water? Did you know that we can thirst for other things too? We can thirst for friendship or success or meaning. But did you know that God is the only one who can truly quench our thirst?

Let's Get into It . . .

I had a season of my life as a single man when I devoted my days to extended time for reading my Bible, listening to the Bible on headphones in the car and at the gym, and setting aside time to pray and listen to God. The more I did it, the more I craved time to be with God and learn about Jesus. I then started a new job that was more time-consuming, began to date, and found I could not spend the same amount of time with God as I had been spending—and I could feel it. It felt like I was not as spiritually hydrated. I was thirsty for time with God.

Let's Learn . . .

There are many ways you can tell you're not drinking enough water. You may feel more tired than usual. Some people who don't drink enough water have joint pain, body aches, and stiffness. Did you know that our spinal discs and cartilage are made up of about 80 percent water? Being hydrated can do wonders for our bodies and help protect our bones from grinding.

Another sign of dehydration is muscle shrinkage, as the majority of our muscles are made up of water. Kids, when you see the Incredible Hulk or other cool muscular heroes, remember that their muscles need water to give their bodies that full-pumped look. And one more thing about water: if it is tough to recover from being sick, you may need to drink more water to flush the toxins out of your system.

There are key signs that let us know if we are getting spiritually dehydrated. When you start to notice you are getting more impatient with your family and friends and with challenging situations, you probably are spiritually dehydrated. When you become more anxious, rude, disobedient, fearful, and quick-tempered, you are probably spiritually dehydrated. Just as with your physical body, there are clues that you need to hydrate spiritually.

The way we hydrate spiritually is by spending time with God. When we fail to do this, we can become spiritually dehydrated, which causes us to respond to people and situations out of our human nature instead of the way God wants us to respond. When we read the Bible, pray, meditate, and listen for the Lord, it's as if we are drinking a cold, refreshing glass of water.

We can temporarily quench our thirst by talking to friends, reading books, playing video games, working out, taking part in our favorite hobbies and activities, talking to counselors, and keeping ourselves busy. And while these things can be helpful, they will not quench our spiritual thirst. When we are feeling physically thirsty, we are already dehydrated, and if we drink coffee, energy drinks, sugary juice boxes, soda, or alcohol, our thirst will not be quenched. In fact, they will make us even thirstier.

You may be in a place right now where you feel like you're doing pretty good and can take care of things on your own without much help from God. Yet you still feel empty inside. That's because God truly is the only one who can quench your thirst. If you make it a point to drink from God's living water daily, you will no longer feel dehydrated, and you will thirst for even more of his refreshing living water.

When you are trying to find temporary happiness in life, remember that God is the living water. Only he can quench your thirst.

Does the idea of living water make sense to you? It's easier to know when you are experiencing physical dehydration, but can you think of ways that show you might be spiritually dehydrated? How can we remind ourselves to drink more of God's living water and to connect with the Lord more when we are feeling the symptoms of spiritual dehydration?

Let's Pray . . .

Dear God,
Thank you that we can never run out of your living water, and that you will always quench our spiritual thirst. Please help us turn to you first when we feel like our well is running dry. Amen.

Let's Act . . .

- Parents, here is your physical and spiritual health challenge for the week: spend at least ten minutes praying and reading your Bible every day. Men, I want to challenge you to drink 3.7 liters (about 125 ounces) of water a day; women, your goal is 2.7 liters (about 91 ounces) of water a day.
- Kids, you have our own physical and spiritual health challenge this week: spend ten minutes a day learning about God and praying. (Parents, you can help them with this.) If you can't read yet, listen to a kids version of the Bible or watch a video or listen to a story about God. Kids one to

three years old should drink at least four cups of water, milk, or almond milk every day. Kids four to eight years old should drink at least five cups of water. Kids ages nine and up should drink at least seven to eight cups of water.

46

EASTER ALIVE AND WELL

"He is not here; he has risen! Remember how he told you, while he was still with you in Galilee: 'The Son of Man must be delivered over to the hands of sinners, be crucified and on the third day be raised again.'"

Luke 24:6–7

Let's Think about It . . .

Do you know why we celebrate Easter? What parts of the Easter story stand out to you? Have you ever wondered how Jesus rose from the grave and ascended into heaven? Do you wonder what it would have been like to live back then and see him? Do you understand why it is important that Jesus is alive and not dead?

As a family, we go to church and worship on Easter. We want to make sure the kids hear the story of Jesus and the reason we celebrate this most important holiday. We also take time to talk about what we learned in church or Bible study. We love to have fun, so we make sure the kids partake in a community Easter egg hunt so they can meet other kids and cheer them on. Then we create our own Easter egg hunt with just the family and hide special prizes in the golden eggs we stash in the grass among the other colored eggs. We want them to know the weight and reality of who Jesus is and what he went through, but we also want them to have fun finding and eating candy as they celebrate their relationship with the God who loves them and brought Jesus back to life!

Let's Learn . . .

I have good news for you. You never have to worry if Jesus Christ your Savior and Lord is alive! We celebrate Easter because it represents how much God loves us. During the Easter season, we take time to remember all that God did for us. We are imperfect human beings who mess up a lot of the time. We don't listen to others, argue with our family and friends, and get into trouble because of our actions. Despite this, God cares so much about us that he sent his one and only Son, who was perfect, to give up his life as a sacrifice so we could receive life with Christ for eternity. Jesus' death on the cross allows us to ask for forgiveness when we mess up or do not represent Jesus the way we should.

When Jesus lived on earth, he helped people by sharing the good news, feeding them, and healing them. However, there were a lot of mean people who did not like Jesus or believe that he was the Son of God. They made fun of him, hurt him, and hung him on a cross to die.

[Parents, take time to answer any questions your kids may have at this point. If they wonder what hanging on a cross means, explain it in a way appropriate for their age. Perhaps you can let them know that crucifixion was a punishment reserved for bad people who did bad things. Although Jesus had done nothing wrong, he still accepted the cruel punishment out of his deep love for us.]

This was a very sad day for Jesus and his friends. Jesus was innocent, but he still had to endure the punishment. While he hung on the cross, after a period of time Jesus stopped breathing and died. He was taken down from the cross by his friends and lovingly wrapped in clean linen and buried in a tomb. Because the Pharisees remembered that Jesus had said he would rise from the dead on the third day (see Luke 18:31–33), the guards had rolled a stone in front of the tomb. The stone weighed somewhere between two and four thousand pounds, which would have made it impossible for even a strong man to move the rock himself, let alone a man who had been badly beaten and hung on a cross to die.

On that third day, an earthquake took place and an angel came down and removed that stone, allowing Jesus to walk out of the tomb. The soldiers who were guarding the tomb were so scared that they fainted and fell down. Jesus' friends were so happy to see that he had risen! Jesus was alive! That is why we celebrate Easter. Jesus died and rose again, and he is alive and well. He gave us the ultimate gift in his resurrection. That is why we celebrate, honor, and worship him.

Jesus is alive! The Easter story shows us how much God loves us. He sent his Son to die for our sins, and he rose again. Because of this, we can have eternal life.

Let's Talk about It . . .

How can we make Jesus a central part of our Easter celebration? How can the way we live show gratitude to Jesus for making a way for us to live with him in heaven one day? How can we share the good news of Easter with others so they will know about and trust in Jesus too?

Let's Pray . . .

Dear God,
Thank you for the Easter story! Thank you that it's not just a story—that Jesus truly died on the cross for our sins and rose again on the third day. Help us to know this is true and to tell others about the gift of salvation and the new life you give us. Amen.

Let's Act . . .

- As a family, read the Easter story together and spend some time discussing these questions:

  1. Why did Jesus die on the cross?
  2. Why did the guards roll a stone in front of Jesus' tomb?
  3. How was the stone removed?
  4. What day did Jesus rise from the dead?
  5. To whom did Jesus first appear? What did he say?

47

IMAGE ISSUES

Your beauty should not come from outward adornment, such as elaborate hairstyles and the wearing of gold jewelry or fine clothes. Rather, it should be that of your inner self, the unfading beauty of a gentle and quiet spirit, which is of great worth in God's sight.

1 Peter 3:3–4

Let's Think about It . . .

How often do you look in the mirror and notice your flaws? Do you have goals you are trying to reach physically? Do you think those goals are realistic? Do you think your environment, social media, friends, or family impact how you view yourself? Do you ever wish you looked a little different? If so, why? If not, that's a great thing—please try to keep this healthy mentality throughout your life.

My daughter had just had her hair braided and it looked really cool. When my wife took the braids out, my daughter's hair was curly and full of volume. I came around the corner and saw her in the kitchen and immediately said, "Wow, you look beautiful! I love your hair. You should wear it like that." She replied, "Thanks, Dad, but I'm not going to wear my hair like this." I asked, "Why not?" She said she felt her hair was too poufy. I thought to myself, *Where did she learn that, and why does poufy hair seem like such a negative thing?*

My daughter's environment had made her insecure about the way her hair naturally looked, which affected the way she viewed herself. What is sad is that she was only five years old. Image issues start young, and if we don't teach our kids how God views them and show them what truly matters, they will go through life spiritually weak and easily discouraged by the world's standards of beauty.

We are to honor the bodies we have been given. It is our duty to treat ourselves well and to preserve the temple (our body) to the best of our abilities. The things we consume on a daily basis play a huge part in how we look, feel, and act. Having confidence in who you are and choosing not to care about the beauty standards set by our culture are a difficult fight for nearly everyone.

We all want to be admired. We all want to look good and feel confident in our skin. However, that's only a small part of the overall picture. I don't eat nutritious foods and work out just because I want to be healthy on the inside. To be honest, I would love to eat all the starchy food, fast food, cookies, ice cream, donuts, and sweets I wanted if I knew these foods would not make me gain weight and look unhealthy on the outside. I work out to look good for my own selfishness as well. However, I also ultimately want to be healthy from the inside out so I can live a long, healthy life and be around for a long time for my family.

We become truly beautiful when our hearts radiate with God's love. There is nothing more attractive than a person who is beautiful from the inside out. When someone looks attractive on the outside but is ugly on the inside, it makes them unappealing. Kids, you will be told a lot of false ideas about what beauty looks like, so I'm going to give you a peek into what the Bible says that will help you to be strong, confident, and beautiful from the inside out. We should all have the goal of achieving the everlasting quality of a gentle and quiet spirit, which is of great worth in God's sight. God wants us to be nice to people and treat others with care, respect, love, admiration, and honor as we serve as many of God's people as possible.

You are God's child, and he loves you dearly. When you feel like you're "less than," it's okay to tell God how you feel. You won't feel great about yourself all the time—and that's normal. No matter how we look—curly hair, straight hair, thin hair, thick hair, bald, short, tall, skinny, stocky, dark skin, light skin—we will always feel insecure about something. But God created each of us, and he is pleased with the way every one of us looks. Put your main effort into working on what is on the inside, and that will radiate beauty on the outside.

Even though God loves how you look (after all, he created you!), he does not value your worth based on your outward appearance. What is on the inside is most important to him, and he loves and values you, no matter what.

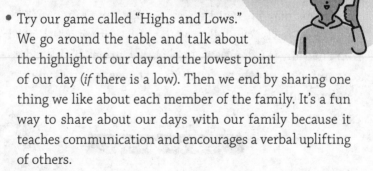

Are you hard on yourself about how you look? Do you think God wants us to live that way? Nobody in this world is perfect, so how can we focus more on what's on the inside. How can we know if our outward appearance is taking over our lives? When we are tempted to feel inferior or unworthy, how can we remind ourselves of who we truly are?

Let's Pray . . .

Dear God,
Thank you for creating each of us in such a unique way. We are honored that you made us unlike anyone else on the planet. Please help us appreciate and love who you created us to be. Teach us how to have a gentle, sweet, and quiet spirit from the inside out. Amen.

Let's Act . . .

- Try our game called "Highs and Lows." We go around the table and talk about the highlight of our day and the lowest point of our day (*if* there is a low). Then we end by sharing one thing we like about each member of the family. It's a fun way to share about our days with our family because it teaches communication and encourages a verbal uplifting of others.
- Have each family member share one *internal* quality that they like about each person to encourage the family to avoid focusing on one another's external appearance.

⋟48⋞

OPEN HOUSE

> My dear brothers and sisters, take note of this: Everyone should be quick to listen, slow to speak and slow to become angry.
>
> **James 1:19**

? Let's Think about It . . .

Parents, is it hard for you to listen to your kids, spouse, family, or other people in general without reacting? Would you like your kids to be better about sharing with you, but you suspect your reactions may prevent them from opening up more? Kids, do you feel like you can talk to your parents about anything? Have you had any problems at school or in your neighborhood or online or anywhere else that you haven't yet told your parents about?

Let's Get into It . . .

My son came home from school one day and told me a boy in his class had pushed him and grabbed his hair. Before he could finish the story, I was asking him a bunch of questions: "Why did he do that? Are you okay? What did you do to him? Did you hit him back?" Then I caught myself, realizing I needed to slow down. I needed to be quick to listen but slow to speak—and even slower to get angry. I can't help but want to protect my son, but this is exactly why God told us how to react to a situation or a person. He will give us direction and guide our next steps if we let him speak to us through his Word and through the Holy Spirit.

Let's Learn . . .

As we strive to become closer as families, our aim should be to create spaces of comfort, trust, honesty, and openness. We should all desire to know more about each other. There is still so much I don't know about my wife, and we have been married for eleven years. And there is so much she doesn't know about me too. We enjoy talking to each other and sharing our thoughts and our hearts about so many topics. However, we must keep in mind that our dreams, desires, aspirations, and goals sometimes change.

As we grow closer, my wife and I want to feel comfortable sharing anything on our heart with each other—both the easy things and the tough things. When you throw in the family dynamic of having extra humans who live in the house and take up space rent-free, that can get tricky. A lot of the alone time you had before having those beautiful babies starts to disappear. Plus, you need to create a space for the kids to feel comfortable enough to share their own heart, daily experiences, and thoughts without judgment. It can be a tricky balance.

Parents, we want our children to feel comfortable sharing things without us freaking out. If we start when they are young to make judgment-free sharing a normal way of life, we are setting the foundation for a beautiful relationship. Kids, you are loved so very much. That's why you are going through this devotional with your family. I want you to feel comfortable telling your parents, guardians, or grandparents anything. It isn't healthy to hold your pain inside, keep your happiness to yourself, or hide your dreams.

My desire for your family is that you be close to one another. I pray that the bonds that develop when your kids are young will be special all the days of your lives. I hope your kids will always feel comfortable talking to you, from the shallowest of conversations to the deepest, jaw-dropping topics you will need to pray about and navigate through together. I pray that God will always remain the center of your family relationship.

> God wants us to be quick to listen and
> slow to speak and slow to become angry.
> This is the best way to control our
> reactions and improve our relationships.

Let's Talk about It . . .

How do you work to create a culture of openness in your home? Are you aware of how you react or respond to situations? Or are you a poor listener who cuts the other person off just to prove a point. What new practices could we implement that would help us listen better and be more Christlike as we connect with one another?

Dear God,
Help us live humbly and learn how to stop trying
to control everything. We want to be a family that
exudes humility, patience, and kindness. Bless our
home and help it to be a safe place where we can have open
conversations that offer the confidence to share our hearts
with one another. Amen.

Let's Act . . .

- When you are looking for a new home
and visit an open house, you can walk
through all the rooms and see the entire
house. Nothing is closed off, and no rooms are a surprise.
Your family home should be like an open house where
everything is in view and it is safe to share your heart,
trust your family, not be judged, be honest, and be slow
to speak and even slower to get angry. As a family, think
of some ways you can make your home a more welcoming
place so everyone feels cozy and comfortable and accepted.

Sometimes cleaning up your physical home can actually help you clean up your heart. Consider . . .

- decluttering your home so it's easier to keep clean and you don't spend more time taking care of stuff than taking care of one another;
- posting Bible verses or artwork with inspirational sayings throughout your home;
- allowing kids access to all the common spaces in your home and not just limiting them to their rooms or a playroom;

- keeping favorite snacks and drinks on hand—popcorn, favorite fruits and veggies with dip, hot tea, cocoa—so parents and kids can sit down together for a snack and chat session; and
- making welcoming outdoor spaces for family relaxation and fun.

⇒49⇐

SAY NO TO ARGUMENTS

A gentle answer turns away wrath,
but a harsh word stirs up anger.

Proverbs 15:1

? Let's Think about It . . .

How often do arguments take place in your family? Mom versus dad? Parents versus kids? Brother versus sister? How does your family resolve the conflict? Do you argue with people outside of your family? How do you resolve those arguments? Would you like to understand how you can apply God's Word and prevent arguments before they even get going?

Let's Get into It . . .

My wife and I are no strangers to a good ole argument. We both have strong personalities, and sometimes we let the stresses of life stir up our wrath. We are not proud of our arguments, and we don't get into disagreements often. However, we all need reminders that everyone is susceptible

to weakness and that the devil likes to stir up wrath, create confusion, and create obstacles to keep us from carrying out God's plan.

Let's Learn . . .

Satan does not like families. The more he can distract us from our unity as a family and create division, the more he wins. But when we learn how to control our emotions, we can save our marriages, families, and relationships. When we allow pride, lack of self-control, hurtful words, or anger to be our guide, we have the potential to ruin families and hurt kids.

Sometimes failed marriages and broken families can cause children to turn against God. This is exactly what Satan wants to happen. When we allow reckless words to flow from our mouths, they can hurt other people and result in failed marriages, broken friendships, and fractured relationships between family members.

I love today's Scripture verse because it simplifies how we should approach an argument and reminds us of who we are as Christians. We are to operate out of humility and use our words to speak life and bless others. Now, keep in mind that this is easier said than done because in the heat of the moment we often choose to react from our old patterns rather than let the Holy Spirit step in and help us respond with gentle and kind words.

Did you know it is impossible to argue with someone who refuses to argue? If kids could learn from a young age the importance of not needing to prove a point, they would gain more control over their emotions and have fewer problems. When we lose control of our emotions as we try to gain control over someone else, we are doomed to failure. When we argue without boundaries, when we say things that are impossible to take back, people can get hurt.

We need to think before we speak. The way we talk to our brothers, sisters, friends, neighbors, coworkers, children, parents, and spouses reveals a lot about who we are and what our relationship with Christ is like. Proverbs 11:12 says, "Whoever derides their neighbor has no sense, but the one who has understanding holds their tongue." Parents, we need to remember that our children watch us and listen to everything we say. They know when we are arguing, and it doesn't feel good or build their confidence in us.

It is usually better to take a time-out and not say anything at all instead of saying everything you are thinking. When you have calmed down and feel like you can have a civil conversation, then resume your discussion. Your family is special. If you cultivate it, tend to it, and treat it with care, your family can minister to many other people who also want to have a beautiful family. Saying no to arguments and choosing to speak words of kindness can save your family from a lot of heartache and help you—and others—grow closer to God.

Psalm 94:16 says, "Who will rise up for me against the wicked? Who will take a stand for me against evildoers?" The only form of "arguing" that God accepts is our defending of the gospel.

Let's Talk about It . . .

Brainstorm ideas that will help you think before you speak and help you control your tongue. How have you seen others use their words to encourage and uplift you? How can that help you practice the same skills?

Let's Pray . . .

Dear God,
Thank you for the gift of words. Help us use our
words for good, not for evil. Help us speak words
that will encourage and help others. Please guide us
in healthy ways to avoid arguments and to build a
closer family. Amen.

Let's Act . . .

- Memorize Proverbs 15:1 as a family
this week. You can create artwork with
the verse on it and display it in your home.
Allow it to help you pay careful attention to your words, to
stop yourself and pray rather than complain or argue and
to speak words of kindness instead.

50

LOVE OVER FEAR

For I am the LORD your God
who takes hold of your right hand
and says to you, Do not fear;
I will help you.

Isaiah 41:13

Let's Think about It . . .

How do you know God is by your side? Does it sometimes feel like he isn't around? Have you ever felt afraid? What are some things you are afraid of? What about trying something for the first time? Is that scary? How would you feel if you knew God was always with you?

Let's Get into It . . .

I came across the Paralympian track star David Brown on TikTok one day, and I was completely blown away by what I saw. David is considered the world's fastest completely blind sprinter. Diagnosed with Kawasaki disease as a baby, he lost all of his vision by the age of thirteen. He says he lived most of his life in fear until he started running.

When I saw David on TikTok, I noticed he ran with something tied around his eyes and someone running very close beside him. As I looked closer, I realized he was running alongside a guy who is called a "sighted guide." David and his guide were connected by a piece of rope tied around each of their wrists. I couldn't imagine the athleticism it took to run next to someone without drifting toward the other person and tripping each other up.

In the videos, David and his sighted guide were running so fast that it looked like they were floating. However, what stuck out the most was how David overcame his fear and trusted his guide to lead him safely across the finish line. David is completely blind and cannot see where he is going, but he has put his complete trust in his sighted guide to be with him the entire way. It's important to remember that David's guide is human. At any given time, he can make a mistake. He can stumble, get injured, or get out of sync with David and cause him harm. Yet David still trusts him.

Let's Learn . . .

Just as David's guide is with him in every step of the race, God is with you every step in the race of life. God will never let you down. He is holding your hand when you are feeling lost, afraid, hurt, worried, or lonely. When you feel abandoned by your friends or family or anyone else, God is right there to hold you in his arms and comfort you. When fear wants to creep up on you, God is there. All throughout the Bible, he commands us to not fear and promises to strengthen us, help us, and be by our side.

When you feel scared, God is with you! God is almighty and powerful. There is no match for God, and he is on your team.

That should make you feel good! God loves you so much, and he wants the best for you. You may go through tough times and deal with difficult situations, but that doesn't mean God has abandoned you. These circumstances will only make you stronger. You will be a better kid, mom, dad, brother, sister, friend, and believer of God when you make it to the other side of the journey.

If David Brown can trust another person—an incredibly talented human being but still a human being—to guide him across the finish line, how much more should we trust God with our lives? Don't give fear any strength in your life. When you feel fear setting in, that's when you call on the name of Jesus and say, "I can do all things through Christ who gives me strength." God loves you so much that he will always be by your side, every step of the way.

We fear a lot of things in this world. But God is always there to take away our fear and to help us through any situation.

Let's Talk about It . . .

Describe a time you overcame fear and became stronger in your faith. How can we grow in our trust that God is with us in every situation in our lives right now and that he won't leave us?

Let's Pray . . .

Dear God,
Thank you that your love overcomes all fear. When I am scared or worried, help me remember that you already have everything all figured out and that you will guide me safely across the finish line of life. Amen.

Let's Act . . .

- It can be really hard to talk about our fears. Sometimes we think that if we ignore them, they will just go away. But that doesn't always work. Sometimes we do need to talk about them and deal with them so we can face them with courage and overcome them. Gather together as a family and take time to discuss these questions. Really listen to each other and don't discount anyone's fears. Then pray together. (It will be powerful to speak Isaiah 41:13 over each other.)

1. What things [people, situations, imagined fears] scare you?
2. Why do they scare you?
3. Do you believe God is with you all the time?
4. What is the biggest fear you are dealing with right now?
5. How can others help you overcome this fear?

51

ANGER

> Get rid of all bitterness, rage and anger, brawling and slander, along with every form of malice. Be kind and compassionate to one another, forgiving each other, just as in Christ God forgave you.
>
> **Ephesians 4:31–32**

Let's Think about It . . .

Are you angry about something right now? Do you struggle with anger? Is it hard for you to let things go when you are upset, or does letting go of anger come easily to you? Do you tend to throw a fit or get frustrated when things don't go your way or you can't figure something out, or is it in your nature to stay calm?

Let's Get into It . . .

Let me tell you the story of a bad day. I wake up early in the morning and stub my toe on the way to the restroom. I then hit my eye on the corner of the wall and split my eyelid. Because I have to clean up the blood and tend to the wound, I end up running late for work. I quickly shower, get dressed, and rush out of the house, only to find that it is sleeting, which leads to a bunch of freaked-out drivers creating slow-moving traffic on my way to work.

After I sit in traffic, getting increasingly more frustrated and annoyed, I get to work, where my boss confronts me with a problem that needs attention. Mentally, I am not ready for this drama because I have had an eventful morning and my emotions are close to being out of control. At this point, though, everything is starting to annoy and frustrate me. Bitterness starts to set in, and I am about to miss out on what God may have for me because the day starts off so badly. (Can you relate?)

Let's Learn . . .

We all have days when it feels like nothing is going right. During these moments, I sometimes wish I could do an adult version of what my two-year-old does when she gets upset. She throws her head back, tilts her face to the clouds, and starts screaming like Godzilla at the top of her lungs. Then with her shoulders slumped in distress, she continues to whine until we calm her down. When little kids have days like this, it can get out of hand quickly because they are not yet mature enough to solve problems on their own. We have to help them get to the root of the problem and calm them down before chaos ignites.

I know issues can get a little toasty between family members at times. However, the Bible tells us we must do our best to get rid of bitterness (which includes resentment), holding on to wrongs, anger, rage (a verbal outpouring of our angry feelings), shouting, slander, and malice. We have experienced all these things in some form or fashion.

When kids have these feelings, they act on them, and we have to address their behavior at the root and teach them there are other ways to cope. As adults, we must not speak to each other with malice and meanness or yell at our spouses or our kids. These actions are rooted in evil and do not uplift our families, coworkers, friends, people we encounter on social media, video gamers we connect with on headsets, or even other drivers on the road.

Each day we can work on becoming more like Christ, which requires being patient, praying, spending time with the Lord, and being intentional. Kids, when you feel yourself getting upset and mad, ask God to help you fix your attitude. God does not want us to be wild, rude, resentful, or mean. He does not want us to be troublemakers in school, at home, in our neighborhoods, or in any other place. God's light in us should shine brightly, and the desire to be a kind person should pierce the darkness of anger and other harmful emotions.

> **God does not want us to let harmful emotions get the best of us. He wants us to be kind and compassionate toward one another and have a forgiving heart.**

Let's Talk about It . . .

Do you see your own natural instinct, when things go wrong, to get upset and take out your anger on others? Why do you think God doesn't want us to live like that? How have you seen others be kind and compassionate, loving and forgiving to you? Do you believe that God can help you do that as well?

Dear God,
When nothing seems to go right, it is easy to get
frustrated and let our emotions spiral out of control.
Help us stay calm when things go wrong and trust
you to make things better. Amen.

Let's Act . . .

- Look at Ephesians 4:31–32 together as a family and discuss the following questions:
    1. What six things did Paul say needed to be removed from us as Christians?
    2. Why should we be compassionate to others?
    3. Are you dealing with any anger, bitterness, or malice? If so, you can pray about it—right now together.
- If the kids in our family have a heated debate or argument among themselves, we separate them and give them a time-out to cool off. Then we have them apologize and ask for forgiveness, and the other person has to respond. Then we ask them to hug it out. Talk through how your family could incorporate some of our ideas, or come up with your own!

52

NO DOUBT

When you ask, you must believe and not doubt, because the one who doubts is like a wave of the sea, blown and tossed by the wind. That person should not expect to receive anything from the Lord. Such a person is double-minded and unstable in all they do.

James 1:6–8

? Let's Think about It . . .

What are you asking God for right now? Is it hard to believe God can make it happen? Do you tend to lead with your emotions, or are you more logical about your belief? Is it difficult to ask God for things? Or is it easy to ask him and trust he will do what he says he will do?

While we were living in Charlotte, North Carolina, my wife and I began to feel like our time there was ending. We had just found out my wife was pregnant with our fourth child. We had no family in North Carolina and had been wanting to move closer to family. We started to look into the possibility of moving back to Seattle, Washington, but we weren't sure how we were going to make it happen. So we prayed together and asked God that if moving was what he wanted for us in this next season of life, would he please make that clear to us. He did just that.

Let's Learn . . .

Some seasons of life are confusing, and it's easy to lose faith during those times. The particular season of life my family was in—trying to decide if we should move to Seattle or stay in Charlotte—was tough. We had moved to North Carolina for a job, but the job hadn't worked out and we were living in a place where we barely knew anyone. On top of that, we were strapped for cash and weren't sure we could even pay for a move. I knew we were supposed to trust God and prepare to move back to Seattle if God opened that door. Our kids were getting excited about the idea of moving back to the West Coast and being closer to Grammie, my wife's mother.

However, a tiny bit of doubt had started to creep in. I started sending résumés to places in both Charlotte and in Washington. I knew in my heart that I didn't need to apply for jobs in Charlotte because we were not going to stay. However, I told my wife I would apply to jobs in both places just to see what would work out. I kept getting responses from places in Washington, but none of them paid the salary we were looking for. During my prayer time, though, God reminded me to ask in faith without doubting.

I should not have doubted God. If we trust him fully, he will do the rest. Things immediately started to change—all within hours of my prayer time. The gym we were a part of told me about a job offer in Charlotte and another in Washington. The woman at the gym in Charlotte told me, "We would love to hire you or we would be happy to reach out to the manager in Washington for you. Talk to your wife about it. Whichever one you choose, I'll either make the call to Washington or start the interview process here in Charlotte." When I went home to talk to my wife, we decided we were officially on the same page—without any doubt and with a lot of faith, we chose the gym in Washington.

We did not know how things would work out; we just knew God was going to make the best thing happen. I love being in this position, because then we are doing our part in making plans while also being sensitive enough to the Spirit that we respond to God's commands. He wants our full trust. And he wants families to have full trust together—to be in agreement with God and with each other.

As soon as we fully trusted God with the moving process, everything started to fall into place. I went through the interview process and was hired, and within months we were out of our lease in Charlotte, packed, and ready to move to the Pacific Northwest. The timing was amazing because I started my job on March 1, 2020, and twelve days later, the pandemic hit. God knew we needed to be around family during that time, and just a couple months later, our baby, Ava Joy, was born on May 22, 2020.

I'm so thankful we serve a God who cares about every detail of our lives. And I'm thankful we can put our full trust in him.

God does not want us to doubt him. The key is having faith, and that is why we must learn to trust God for everything.

Let's Talk about It . . .

How have you doubted God recently? How can you put your faith in him instead? How can we build up our trust in God and be reminded of his promises to help and be a good Father?

Let's Pray . . .

Dear God,
Thank you that when it comes to you and your plans for us, we don't have to doubt you at all. Please help our family to put our complete trust in you and have faith that you will do what is best for us. Amen.

Let's Act . . .

- Cut up some pieces of paper or card stock. On each piece of paper, write down something you want to trust God with—family, finances, decisions, friendships, faith, anything at all. Put the pieces of paper in a jar and spend time this week drawing one out and praying for that particular thing and the family member who wrote it down.
- What does your family need right now? Write down a list of what your family is praying for—a new job for a parent, healing for a grandparent, good friends for the kids, a good church where you can learn about Jesus, opportunities to

tell more people about God. Spend time praying for these things, and be sure to write down when and how God answers your prayers. Have faith that God will always lead you to what is best for you. He may not answer your prayers in the way you imagined he would, but his plan is always the best thing.

ACKNOWLEDGMENTS

I truly believe in quality over quantity. Having quality influence in your life is more beneficial than a plethora of voices in your circle. I want to thank every single one of you who helped shape, support, and inspired me to write this book. If your name isn't in here and you played a part, you know who you are, and your humility to not be in it is admirable.

To my mom, Deborah Dooley, thank you for being a mother who always told me to dream big, keep God first, and live life with outlandish faith. To my brother Allen Dooley, I'm believing in a miracle for you—love you, bro!

Lewis Shine II, I'm excited that we are living out some of our conversations from Peabody Hall in college. Thank you for being my longest-standing best friend. Love you, bro!

Mom Donna, thank you for being the best mother-in-law I could only dream of. Your support and belief in me push me to be a better person. Papa T, thank you for supporting me. You are so instrumental in my writing process.

Fetu and Elizabeth, you played such a huge part in my process to help kick off my writing. I can't thank you enough for providing space for me to write. You guys are some of the most generous people I know. I appreciate you dearly.

Justine and Kim, I'm so blessed to have inherited such amazing sisters. Thank you for your continued prayers and your faith. You guys are overcomers!

Thank you so much for believing in me, Kathleen Ortiz. I'm

so grateful I have you on my team, and you are truly a genius go-getter. I'm honored to have you in my corner.

Barnes & Noble at the Village at Totem Lake, Kirkland, Washington, has some of the coolest employees on the planet. Thank you for allowing me to write the majority of my book in your store for countless hours. Also, I'll never forget how you made my contract signing with Zondervan so special.

Finally, I want to thank the amazing team at Zondervan that has provided incredible support. Carolyn McCready, you are one of the most kindhearted people I've come into contact with. I am forever grateful for this opportunity, and I don't take it lightly. I look forward to more in the future.